CAMBRIDGE LIBRARY COLLECTION

Books of enduring scholarly value

Religion

For centuries, scripture and theology were the focus of prodigious amounts of scholarship and publishing, dominated in the English-speaking world by the work of Protestant Christians. Enlightenment philosophy and science, anthropology, ethnology and the colonial experience all brought new perspectives, lively debates and heated controversies to the study of religion and its role in the world, many of which continue to this day. This series explores the editing and interpretation of religious texts, the history of religious ideas and institutions, and not least the encounter between religion and science.

Select Narratives of Holy Women: Translation

The twin sisters Agnes Lewis (1843–1926) and Margaret Gibson (1843–1920) were pioneering biblical scholars who became experts in a number of ancient languages. Travelling widely in the Middle East, they made several significant discoveries, including one of the earliest manuscripts of the Four Gospels in Syriac, a dialect of Aramaic, the language probably spoken by Jesus himself. Their chief discoveries were made in the Monastery of St. Catherine on Mount Sinai. This fascicule is the translation of a Syriac manuscript from the monastic library of St. Catherine. Translated by Lewis and first published in 1900, the manuscript recounts the tales of a number of saintly women, including Pelagia, a rich courtesan who converted to Christianity and Eugenia, a holy woman who lived as a man and became the abbot of a monastery. An interesting collection of stories with relevance for scholars of Middle Eastern Christianity.

Cambridge University Press has long been a pioneer in the reissuing of out-of-print titles from its own backlist, producing digital reprints of books that are still sought after by scholars and students but could not be reprinted economically using traditional technology. The Cambridge Library Collection extends this activity to a wider range of books which are still of importance to researchers and professionals, either for the source material they contain, or as landmarks in the history of their academic discipline.

Drawing from the world-renowned collections in the Cambridge University Library and other partner libraries, and guided by the advice of experts in each subject area, Cambridge University Press is using state-of-the-art scanning machines in its own Printing House to capture the content of each book selected for inclusion. The files are processed to give a consistently clear, crisp image, and the books finished to the high quality standard for which the Press is recognised around the world. The latest print-on-demand technology ensures that the books will remain available indefinitely, and that orders for single or multiple copies can quickly be supplied.

The Cambridge Library Collection brings back to life books of enduring scholarly value (including out-of-copyright works originally issued by other publishers) across a wide range of disciplines in the humanities and social sciences and in science and technology.

Select Narratives
of Holy Women:
Translation

From the Syro-Antiochene or Sinai Palimpsest

TRANSLATED BY AGNES SMITH LEWIS

CAMBRIDGE UNIVERSITY PRESS

Cambridge, New York, Melbourne, Madrid, Cape Town,
Singapore, São Paolo, Delhi, Mexico City

Published in the United States of America by Cambridge University Press, New York

www.cambridge.org
Information on this title: www.cambridge.org/9781108043182

This edition first published 1900
This digitally printed version 2012

ISBN 978-1-108-04318-2 Paperback

SELECT NARRATIVES

OF

HOLY WOMEN

𝔏onlon: C. J. CLAY AND SONS,

CAMBRIDGE UNIVERSITY PRESS WAREHOUSE,

AVE MARIA LANE.

𝔊lasgolv: 50, WELLINGTON STREET.

𝔏eipzig: F. A. BROCKHAUS.

𝔑elv 𝔜ork: THE MACMILLAN COMPANY.

𝔅ombap: E. SEYMOUR HALE.

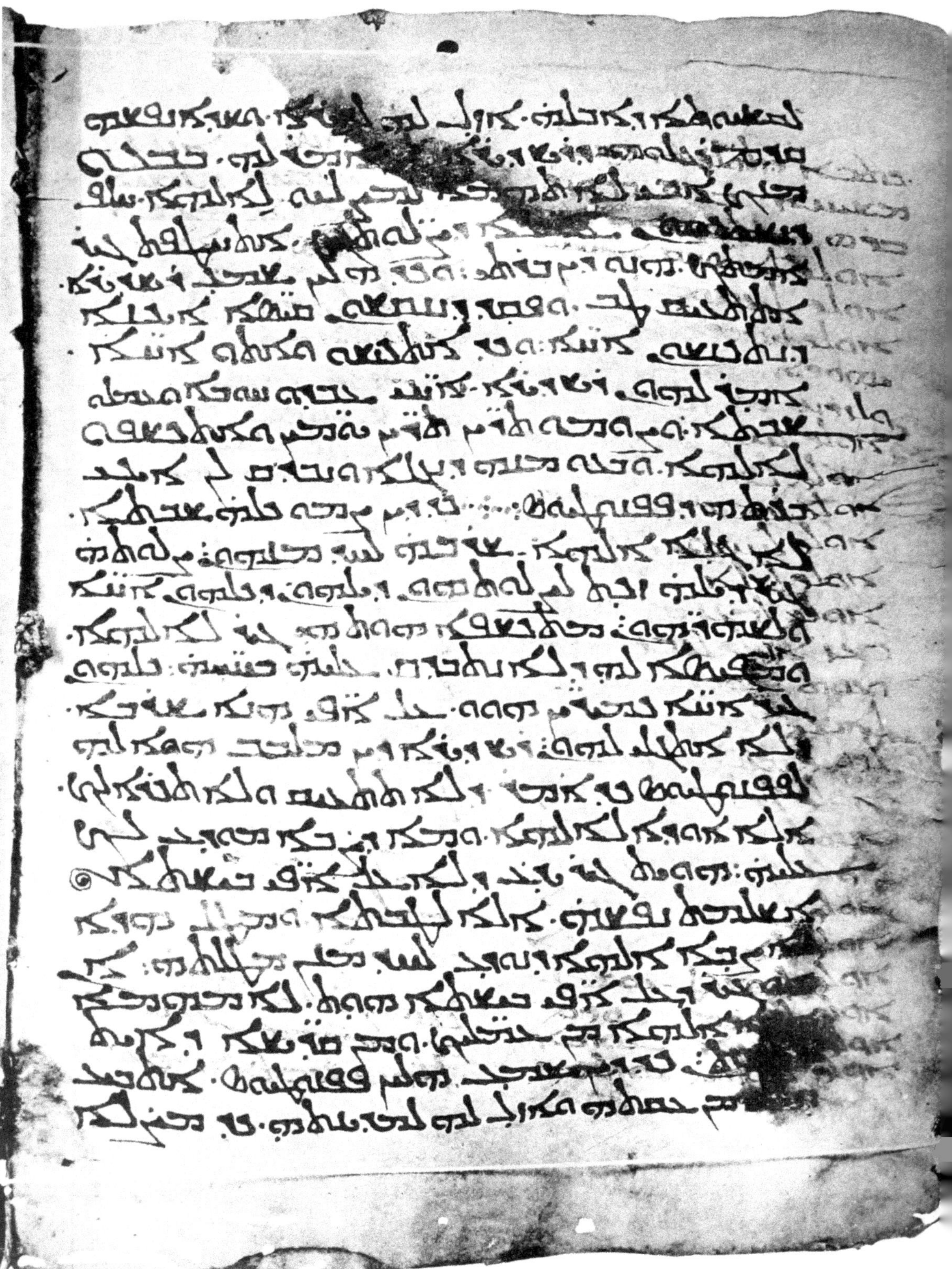

FOL. 82[b]

(Matt. i. 1—17[a] script. inf.)

STUDIA SINAITICA No. X

SELECT NARRATIVES

OF

HOLY WOMEN

FROM

THE SYRO-ANTIOCHENE OR SINAI PALIMPSEST

AS WRITTEN ABOVE THE OLD SYRIAC GOSPELS BY JOHN
THE STYLITE, OF BETH-MARI-QANŪN IN A.D. 778

TRANSLATED BY

AGNES SMITH LEWIS M.R.A.S.

HON. PHIL. DR. HALLE-WITTENBERG

TRANSLATION

LONDON
C. J. CLAY AND SONS
CAMBRIDGE UNIVERSITY PRESS WAREHOUSE
AVE MARIA LANE
1900

Cambridge:

PRINTED BY J. AND C. F. CLAY,
AT THE UNIVERSITY PRESS.

PREFACE.

THIS volume is so closely associated with No. IX. of this series that it hardly requires a separate Preface. The Introductory Notes which precede it belong quite as much to No. IX. as to No. X.; and they have been made to accompany the English Translation, rather than the Syriac Text, with the view of equalizing the size of the two volumes. I shall therefore only recapitulate that these "Select Narratives" form the upper script of the Palimpsest which I discovered in the Convent of St Catharine on Mount Sinai in A.D. 1892, and that the under script is the now famous Codex of the Old Syriac Gospels. Whether the tales are in any way worthy of their position, the reader must judge for himself.

A. S. L.

CONTENTS.

ERRATA.

Page 86, line 26. *For* "Diocletian" *read* "Hadrian."

  ,, 122, ,, 10. *For* "Magdo" *read* "Magedo."

  ,, 140, footnote. *For* Συναξαρίστης *read* Συναξαριστής.

INTRODUCTORY NOTES.

THECLA.

The story of St Thecla is one of the oldest of Christian legendary romances, for it was composed in the beginning of the third century by an Asiatic presbyter, as Tertullian tells us[1], "out of love to St Paul." The Ebionite heretics had sought to calumniate the character of the great Apostle, finding more than one supposed allusion to his fair disciple in the First Epistle to the Corinthians[2], and the best antidote to these aspersions was a tale, wherein the acts of this first of women martyrs were placed in their true light[3].

St Jerome alludes to Thecla as to a real person. He says that after her temptation at Antioch she was prohibited by St Paul from accompanying him any further[4]. This, however, does not actually prove her existence, for he may have simply pointed a moral from the romance.

The story tells us that when Paul was preaching in the city of Iconium, a man named Onesiphorus went out to meet him, accompanied by his wife[5], by Zeno, and by the sons of Simon; that he recognised Paul, who was waiting for him on the highway to Lystra, by his personal appearance, which had been

---

[1] *De Baptismo*, cap. 17.   [2] 1 Cor. vii. 34—38; ix. 5.
[3] Baring Gould, *Contemporary Review*, Oct. 1877 (p. 862).
[4] *Ad Oceanum de Vita clericorum.*
[5] In the Syriac Palimpsest her name is given as ܩܠܐܦܝ.

already described to him by Titus. Paul was a man of medium size, with scanty hair, bandy legs, large eyes, eyebrows which met, and a long nose; he was full of grace and mercy, at one time seeming like a man, and at another like an angel. Demas and Hermogenes, coppersmiths, who accompanied Paul, were filled with envy at his friendly greeting to Onesiphorus; but Paul entered the house of the latter, brake bread, and preached about the controlling of the flesh, and about our Lord's resurrection.

Whilst Paul preached a virgin named Thecla, daughter of Theocleia, betrothed to Thamyris, sat at a window which was close to the roof of Onesiphorus's house and listened to his words both by day and by night. She saw many women going in to hear him, but himself she saw not. Her mother, Theocleia, becoming alarmed, sent for Thamyris; but to him she would not even speak. He waxed wroth, and went down to the street, where he met with Demas and Hermogenes, who excited him still further against Paul. Next morning he went to the house of Onesiphorus, accompanied by the chief men of the city and many people with stones. They dragged Paul before Castelus the governor, the whole city accusing him of being a magician, and of corrupting their wives. The Governor questioned Paul, and sent him to prison.

But Thecla in the night-time bribed the door-keeper of her mother's house with her own bracelets, and the gaoler with a mirror of gold, and having thus got access to Paul, she sat at his feet, listening to his teaching and kissing his fetters. Her family and her betrothed having found her there, they informed the Governor, who commanded that both Paul and Thecla should be brought before him. Thecla simply stood and looked at Paul, being quite silent when she was questioned. Then her mother cried out that she must be burnt, as an example to other women. The Governor commanded Paul to be scourged, and Thecla to be burnt in the theatre. When she had been brought out for that purpose she gazed intently on the crowd, in the hope of seeing Paul. And she saw the Lord Jesus, in the likeness of His apostle, sitting by her side. Whilst she gazed at Him He rose and ascended to heaven. The faggots were piled around her by youths and maidens, but she would not burn; a shower of hail and rain extinguished the flames and killed many of the spectators.

Paul in the meantime was fasting after his scourging, with Onesiphorus, his wife and his children, in a sepulchre by the roadside of the Iconians. Paul gave his tunic to a boy, directing him to sell it and buy bread. The boy, meeting Thecla, brought her to Paul, who had been praying for her deliverance. She proposed to cut off her hair, and follow him everywhere. Then Paul sent away Onesiphorus and his family, and went with her and with other people to Antioch. There they met an influential man named Alexander, who fell in love with Thecla, and offered to buy her from Paul. He replied that she did not belong to him. Alexander tried to embrace Thecla in the open street. But she resisted him, tore off his garments, pulled a golden crown from his head and dashed it on the ground, leaving him standing naked. Alexander complained to the Governor, and Thecla was condemned to be thrown to the wild beasts. Thecla begged from the Governor that she should be kept in purity until the sentence was executed. Taking pity on her, he sent her to the house of a rich queen named Tryphæna, who had lately lost her daughter.

Thecla was taken to the theatre, stripped, and exposed to a huge lioness. Tryphæna stood weeping at the door, but the lioness only licked the martyr's hand. Other beasts were let loose, but they would not touch her, and Tryphæna obeying the commands of her own daughter, whom she had seen in a night-vision, took her away, and adopted her. Thecla then prayed for the gift of everlasting life to the daughter of Tryphæna.

Early next morning Alexander himself came to fetch Thecla. She was snatched from the arms of Tryphæna, and was again exposed naked in the theatre. A lioness was brought, but it lay at her feet; a leopard burst, and a bear was killed by the lioness. Then a lion was brought, but he and the lioness fought till both were dead. Whilst other beasts came against her she looked round and saw a pond of water. Invoking the name of the Christ, she leapt into it, as to her baptism. Many evil beasts which were in the water died, whilst a cloud of lightning encompassed her, screening her from view.

Then Alexander brought out two bulls. Thecla was bound between them with ropes, red-hot spits were applied to their thighs, but as the bulls sprang up, a flash of fire consumed the ropes, setting Thecla free. Tryphæna fainted, thinking that Thecla was dead; and this alarmed Alexander, who ran to the Governor, and begged him to release Thecla, and thus save Tryphæna, who was of the family of Cæsar.

Thecla was then brought before the Governor, and when she had confessed her faith in the Christ, he ordered clothes to be brought for her, and all, especially the women, joined in praising God. Tryphæna was converted, with many of her maidens, and Thecla remained eight days in her house, teaching her God's commandments. But the maiden could not forget Paul. She sent messengers to seek for him, and they found him in the city of Myra. She dressed herself like a man, and took many people with her, even some of the queen's maidens, and went to Myra. Paul was astonished, and took her, with her attendants, to the house of Hermæus. There she related all that had befallen her, and after they had prayed for queen Tryphæna, Paul sent her to the city of Iconium with a commission to teach.

Thecla went to the house of Onesiphorus, where she learned that Thamyris was dead, but that her mother Theocleia still lived. She had the satisfaction of trying to persuade her mother to believe in the Christ, then she went to Seleucia, where she taught for some time, and where she died in peace.

The Latin Church commemorates Thecla on Sept. 23rd. She is said to have died in Isauria, or Lycaonia, her native province, and to have been buried at Seleucia, where a magnificent church was built over her remains. The great cathedral of Milan is dedicated to her. But her body is supposed to rest in a chapel formed out of a natural cave in the Convent of St Thecla at Ma'lula in the Lebanon.

The Greek Church commemorates Thecla on the 24th of September, under the titles of Πρωτομάρτυς and Ἰσαπό-στολος.

It also commemorates two other martyrs of the same name, one of them on June 9th, Sept. 6th, and Nov. 20th, slain with the sword, the other on August 19th, slain by a wild beast at Gaza.

An Arabic inscription several centuries old at the back of the first leaf of the famous Codex Alexandrinus (A) of the Greek Bible, states that it was written by the hand of Thecla the martyr[1]. This is translated into Latin by another hand, which Mr Aldis Wright recognizes as Bentley's[2]. To Thecla is also ascribed the beautiful and complete little Psalter, which the monks of St Catherine's Convent on Mount Sinai show as one of their chief treasures. Though it can be read only through a microscope, no mistake has ever been detected on any of its twelve pages. Unfortunately for these traditions, scholars have assigned the Codex Alexandrinus, by the weight of its own internal evidence, to the fifth century.

As the story has already been edited by one of the greatest of Oriental scholars, Dr William Wright of Cambridge, I have only given in Appendix II. a collation of the Syro-Antiochene text on that published by him. The chief differences between

---

[1] See Scrivener-Miller, *Introduction*, p. 98.

[2] *Academy*, April 17th, 1875.

the two texts are that the former one always amplifies the saint's name into "the blessed Lady Thecla."

In Dr Wright's text p. ⲗⲩⲟ a lacuna seems to exist in the sense, and this is filled up by our text on f. 16ᵃ. The form ⲇⲓⲁⲗⲃⲇⲇ⳨ "she tore herself with her nails," on fol. 14ᵇ, is unusual.

EUGENIA.

The story of Eugenia is nearly the same as that in Add. 14,645, and Add. 14,649 of the British Museum MSS.; these being of the 10th and 9th centuries respectively. The Bishop is called ⲱⲁⲩⲗ⳨, not ⲱⲁⲩⲗ⳨, in them both. His name is not mentioned in the Greek Συναξαριστής. In Add. 14,645 Eugenia's brothers are called ⲱⲁⲗⲓⲥⲣ⳨ and ⲱⲁⲗⲁⲥⲱ; in Add. 14,649 ⲱⲓⲃⲁⲥ or ⲱⲁⲗⲓⲥⲣ⳨ and ⲱⲓⲗⲁⲥⲱ, and in the Palimpsest ⳨ⲗⲓⲥⲣ⳨ and ⲱⲗⲓⲙ. In Add. 14,649 the name of her proposed bridegroom is not ⳨ⲓⲗⲁⲟⲣ⳨ but ⳨ⲓⲗⲃⲥⲁⲩ. The names of her parents and of the two eunuchs are the same in all. In Add. 14,649 the man who was sent to depose her father Philip from the office of Eparch is called ⲱⲁⲩⲓⲃ instead of ⲱⲁⲩⲓⲃ.

The martyrdom of Eugenia is commemorated by the ortho-dox Greek Church on December 24th and by the Latin Church on Christmas-Day. Bedjan's text is from Add. 14,649 and Add. 14,645 of the British Museum.

PELAGIA.

The story of Pelagia is supposed to have happened between the years A.D. 449 and A.D. 451. It is as follows:

The Bishop of Antioch in Syria had occasion to summon a council of eight bishops, amongst whom was St Nonnus, with whom was the narrator of the story, the deacon Jacob. They were all lodged in a hospice attached to the church where the bones of St Julian were preserved.

One day whilst the eight bishops were seated before the church door, discussing various affairs, they asked St Nonnus to expound the Word of God. Whilst he was doing so, a rich courtesan passed before them, seated on a richly caparisoned horse, decked with pearls and precious stones, and accompanied by a host of servants. The air was scented by a profusion of aromatics, and the good bishops were astonished at the dazzling beauty of Pelagia, for such was the courtesan's name.

They, however, turned away their faces from the ostentatious sinner. Nonnus fell on his knees and shed abundance of tears. When Pelagia had passed he said to his brethren, " Do ye not admire the beauty of the courtesan?" They did not reply. He then told them that his admiration of her beauty would impel him to seek more earnestly from God for her conversion to a purer life. Having returned to his cell, accompanied by the deacon, he took himself severely to task for his failure to serve God with as much zeal as Pelagia had displayed in her service of the Devil. The day was Saturday, and on Sunday morning (Divine service having been celebrated during the night) Nonnus called Jacob, and told him that he had seen in a dream how he himself was standing near the horns of the altar, and how a black dove, squalid and dirty, flew above him. When the congregation had departed and he had left the church the dove flew near him. He stretched out his hands, and catching it, threw it into the bath of water on the floor of the church. There it was cleansed, the foul odour which had accompanied it disappeared, and it soared up to heaven.

Then St Nonnus with the seven other bishops and Jacob the deacon went to the largest church in Antioch. After the liturgy, the Archbishop sent the archdeacon to St Nonnus with a Gospel and the permission to teach. This Nonnus did, not in words of human wisdom, but by the inspiration of the Holy Spirit; till the floor of the church became wet with the tears of the listeners, amongst whom was Pelagia, who was well known in the city, and who confessed her many sins in an audible voice. When the moment came for the celebration of the sacred mysteries she went out, but commanded two of her servants to remain as spectators, and to watch when Bishop Nonnus should come out, so that they might find out for her where he was lodging. She then wrote a letter to him, in which she professed her deep penitence, reminding him that the Saviour ate and drank with publicans and sinners. He replied that he could not receive a visit from her alone, as he was only a weak man, liable to temptation, but that he was willing to see her in the presence of his brother bishops. When Pelagia had received this letter she hastened to the church of St Julian, where St Nonnus received her with his colleagues. She threw herself on the ground and embraced his feet with tears, throwing dust on her head, and begging for the remission of her sins.

All the bishops and presbyters who were present were moved to tears. Nonnus professed his willingness to baptize her, but said that by the canons of the Church she must have sponsors. Pelagia then with great vehemence and copious tears told him that God would require her soul at his hands if it were lost through his refusal to baptize her; and that he would also be held to be a partaker of the guilt of her future sins, and begged him to admit her, as his divine Master would have done.

Nonnus then sent Jacob to the Archbishop, to ask his permission for Pelagia's baptism, and also that a deaconess should be sent to him. Jacob returned with a Roman lady, the Superior of the deaconesses, who with some difficulty persuaded Pelagia to rise. After due confession and preparation she was baptized, and received the holy sacrament from the hands of Nonnus. She stated that Pelagia was the name given to her by her parents, but that latterly, on account of her many ornaments, she had frequently been called Margarita.

Then the Devil appeared to Nonnus in the form of a black looking man, and showered imprecations upon him for the many thousands whom he had baptized, and had thus delivered from the power of evil; and most of all for abducting his most perfect hope, Pelagia. Receiving no encouragement, the enemy of all good next turned to Pelagia, and upbraided her with ingratitude, pouring out on her the most bitter reproaches. By the advice of Nonnus she made the sign of the cross, and Satan forthwith fled.

Two days later, however, the Devil returned to Pelagia as she was quietly sleeping beside the Roman deaconess, and reminded her of the great wealth which he had procured for her. But she made the sign of the cross, exclaiming, "The Lord rebuke thee!" and awoke the deaconess. Whereupon Satan fled.

On the third day Pelagia gave freedom to all her slaves, and offered all her wealth, which she had won by an evil life, to the discretion of Bishop Nonnus, who bestowed it on the treasurer of the great church at Antioch, with the request that none of it should be allowed to enter the church itself, nor any dwelling of the clergy, nor might it be hoarded in any way, but that it should be at once distributed amongst orphans, widows, and the sick poor.

For seven days Pelagia fasted from food and drink, showing an example of temperance and of chastity. On the eighth day, which was Sunday, she was expected to put off the bridal robes of her baptism, and to put on a woman's ordinary dress. Towards nightfall, however, she went to Bishop Nonnus, and after receiving his blessing, begged him to give her some of his own garments. He accordingly bestowed on her his hair tunic and woollen mantle. During the night she went out in the dress of a man and was never again seen in the city. There was great consternation and grief about her disappearance, but

Nonnus said that she had chosen the good part, like Mary, and a few days later the Archbishop dismissed the bishops, each one returning to his own town.

Three years later the deacon Jacob went on a pilgrimage to the Holy City, and Bishop Nonnus requested him to make enquiry about a eunuch named Pelagius, from whom he might receive much benefit. After he had performed his devotions at the sacred shrines, he succeeded in finding this person in a cell at the summit of the Mount of Olives, and saw in his face something like the features of Pelagia, defaced and withered by long fasting and many vigils. She recognised him; but he was quite unaware of her identity, until hearing of her death a short time afterwards he attended her funeral, and was present along with the bishop and many other holy men when they discovered that she had been a woman. She was buried with great honour, having in her last years enjoyed the reputation of being a saint, and Jacob was thankful that he had received her benediction.

It is interesting to find that while Gildemeister's text states that Jacob prayed and was blest by the sepulchre of our Lord, the Syro-Antiochene Palimpsest says that he prayed and was blest by our Lord in all the places which he visited (near Jerusalem).

Nonnus is mentioned by Theophanes, as being Bishop of Edessa, *Chronographia*, p. 79.

"Κατὰ τοῦτον δὲ τὸν χρόνον," he says, "Νόννος ὁ θεοφόρος ἐποίμαινε τὴν τῶν Ἐδεσσηνῶν Ἐκκλησίαν, ὁ τὴν πρώτην τῶν μιμάδων Ἀντιοχέων τῷ Θεῷ ἀφιερώσας, καὶ ἀντὶ Μαργαριτοῦς πόρνης ἁγίαν αὐτὴν Πελαγίαν παραστήσας τῷ Χριστῷ."

Pelagia is commemorated by the Greek and Latin Churches on Oct. 8.

MARINA.

The story of Mary, otherwise called Marinus, or Marina, is also found in three of the British Museum MSS., Add. 14,649 (9th century), Add. 12,172 (10th century) and Add. 14,722 (Carshuni, 13th century). In these MSS. the tale has not the exordium of the Syriac Palimpsest. It relates that her mother died when she was seven years old. After her admission into the monastery, and the death of her father, she goes on a journey by command of the Abbot, and lodges, not at an inn, but in the house of a believer ܡܗܝܡܢܐ. On returning, she is not allowed to see the Abbot, but is compelled to sit outside the convent, without any opportunity of exculpating herself; and this she does for four years. The story is told with more conciseness than in the Palimpsest; but with less sympathy and fewer picturesque details. It is free from the absurdity of Marina's self-accusation. The handwriting of both is of considerably later date.

Bedjan appears to have made use chiefly of a manuscript from Mesopotamia, date unknown. The Greek Church commemorates this saint on February 12th, and the Latin Church on June 18th. Her relics were brought from Constantinople to Venice in A.D. 1230, and are venerated there in a church which bears her name. The festival of their translation is kept at Venice on July 17th.

EUPHROSYNE.

This story, as told in the Syriac Palimpsest, is almost in the same words as in Add. 14,649 of the British Museum (9th century); Bedjan's text has a collation from the latter, but is chiefly from a paper MS. in Paris of the 13th century. The word ܐܬܒܣ in the penultimate line of f. 82ᵇ of the Palimpsest is probably a singular spelling for ܐܬܒܣ.

The Greek Church commemorates Euphrosyne on September 25th. She has no place in the Calendar of the Latin Church. Her story is also told in Add. 12,172 and R. F. XLIX. of the British Museum (10th century).

ONESIMA.

The story of Onesima is also told in the British Museum MSS. Add. 14,649, Add. 14,650 and R. F. XLIX. There are some slight variations in the tale, for instance the B. M. MSS. make the beasts of the desert sit round the saint from the sixth till the ninth hour, our Palimpsest from the third hour till the ninth. The Palimpsest states that the portress had sat at the door of the convent for 40 years, the B. M. MSS. extend this to 102 years. This is not the only example which these "Select Narratives" furnish of how ancient legends become more wonderful as time rolls onward.

I can find no mention of Onesima in the Συναξαριστής, nor in the Calendar of the Latin Church.

Bedjan's text is from two paper MSS. in Paris of the twelfth century and also from Add. 14,649 of the British Museum.

DRUSIS.

No Syriac manuscript in the British Museum contains the story of Drusis. But there are hymns in her honour in Add. 14,505 and Add. 17,134, the latter being probably, as Dr Wright thinks, in the autograph of the famous Jacob, Bishop of Edessa.

There is also a homily on Drusis by Chrysostom (II. 688). He relates how she found in the furnace a fountain of clear water; and how she ascended to her heavenly Bridegroom purified both by water and by fire. But he says nothing about her being the daughter of Trajan, nor about her being betrothed to Hadrian. We may therefore suppose that while the legend may contain a kernel of truth, these Imperial relationships of the martyr are simply the outgrowths of popular imagination.

Drusis is commemorated by the Greek Church on March 22nd. There is no mention of her in the Calendar of the Latin Church.

BARBARA.

There is no Syriac text of Barbara in the British Museum. But a reference to her relics will be found on p. 194, c. 1, of Dr Wright's Catalogue.

Barbara is commemorated by the Greek Church on December 4th.

The Συναξαριστής tells us that she was martyred during the reign of the Emperor Maximian, who is the Aximus of our tale, and that her father was a Greek.

In a MS. of the British Museum, CCXLVIII. (Egerton 681) we are told that the relics of St Barbara are entombed in a church in a poor Christian town named Camalisk-Gawerkoe, situated about six hours' journey to the southward of Mosul.

St Barbara is commemorated by the Latin Church on December 4th. She was said to have been a scholar of Origen, and she is said by some to have suffered martyrdom at Nicomedia in the reign of Maximinus I. Others aver that she suffered at Heliopolis in Egypt, in the reign of Galerius, about A.D. 306, and this Joseph Assemani considers to be the most authentic.

MARY.

The text of this story is taken from Add. 17,204 in the British Museum, which belongs to the fifth century, and is written in a fine straight Estrangela hand, in two columns, the small stops being in red. There are few diacritical points, except the *seyyame*, and that over the fem. pronom. suffix ܗ. As the text of the Palimpsest is three centuries later, variants from it only are given. The most remarkable of these is the word "three months" for "three days," given as the period during which Mary was imprisoned in her master's house, the longer period being of course in the later manuscript.

The story is also found in Add. 14,649.

I have failed to find it in the Συναξαριστής, although there are of course more illustrious saints of the same name.

St Mary, the slave of Tertullius, is commemorated by the Latin Church on November 1st.

IRENE.

No Syriac text of this story is to be found in the British Museum.

Irene is commemorated by the Greek Church on May 5th.

Other saints of the same name are commemorated on April 16th, June 5th, July 28th, August 13th.

The name of Irene does not occur in the Calendar of the Latin Church.

Tela, or Tela Mauzalet, otherwise called Constantine, in honour of the great Roman Emperor, who rebuilt it in A.D. 350, was situated about fifty miles due east of Edessa (see *Ecc. Hist. of John, Bishop of Edessa*, R. Payne-Smith's translation, p. 437, foot-note).

EUPHEMIA.

There is a hymn in honour of Euphemia in Add. 17,134 of the British Museum.

She is commemorated on July 11th and September 16th. Other saints of the same name being mentioned on January 4th, November 19th, and November 22nd.

She is also commemorated with Thecla on the fourth Friday after the Invention of the Cross. (See Dr Wright's Catalogue, p. 186, col. 2.)

The Latin Church commemorates her on September 16th. Four churches in Constantinople once bore her name, also a very spacious one at Chalcedon, in which the fourth General Council of the Church, that which condemned Eutyches, assembled in A.D. 451. Her relics were transferred to the great church of St Sophia in Constantinople. They are now preserved at Syllebria, a metropolitical see, on the Propontic shore, between Constantinople and Adrianople, but a portion is in the possession of the church of the Sorbonne in Paris.

SOPHIA.

The story of Sophia and her three daughters is found in Add. 17,204, and Add. 14,645. As the former of these belongs to the fifth century, I have given its text, with the variants of that in the Syriac Palimpsest, and where some of its pages are missing, I have given the text of the Palimpsest, with variants from Add. 14,645 (10th century).

Sophia and her three daughters are commemorated by the Greek Church on September 17th.

Other saints of the same name are mentioned on May 22nd, June 4th, September 18th, and December 18th.

The legend of Sophia may possibly have become intended for an allegory of the manner in which the Divine Wisdom, or in other words Christianity, with her three daughters, Faith, Hope, and Love, were received in the capital of the Roman Empire; how their beauty was acknowledged, while they themselves were derided, tortured, and slain; how the death of the body had no real power over them; and how they drew all men's hearts after them, so that their place of execution was a place of triumph both for this world, and for the world which is invisible.

Two grains of truth may be found in the legend: Hadrian's cruelty to the Christians, and the painful nature of his mortal sickness.

The name of this St Sophia does not occur in the Calendar of the Latin Church.

The British Museum contains, besides the text which I have edited, from Add. 17,204, other texts in Add. 14,644 (5th or 6th century), Add. 14,650 (6th or 7th century), and Add. 14,645 (10th century).

Bedjan's text is from Add. 14,645 and Add. 14,644.

THEODOSIA.

The Syriac text of the story of St Theodosia has been edited by Assemani in his *Acta Martyrum Occidentalium*, vol. II., p. 204, and on this I have collated the text of the Syriac Palimpsest. In the fifth year of the persecution, *i.e.* A.D. 307, under Maximinus we are told that a holy virgin of Tyre, twenty-eight years old, saw some confessors of Christianity who had been brought to the Forum of Cæsarea for judgment, and besought for herself an interest in their prayers. She was seized, and brought before the Prefect, who tried to persuade her to sacrifice to the idols. On her refusal she was subjected to atrocious tortures, from which she was at last released by drowning. The confessors, who had been greatly encouraged by her example, were condemned to labour in the mines of Palestine.

The Greek Church commemorates this saint on May 29th. The Latin Church on April 2nd.

THEODOTA.

The Syriac text of this legend has been edited by Assemani in his *Acta Martyrum Occidentalium*, vol. II., p. 221.

In A.D. 318, in the month of September, under the Emperor Licinius, there was a furious persecution of the Christians in the city of Philippi. Agrippa the Prefect had decreed a solemn feast to Apollo, at which all were commanded to sacrifice. A harlot named Theodota refused to do so, and was therefore thrown into prison. Seven hundred and fifty men, admiring her constancy, resolved to abstain from the sacrifice. Theodota was then deprived of both food and drink for twenty-one days; but being again brought before the tribunal she confessed her faith in the Christ; and was condemned by Agrippa to cruel tortures, which included the extraction of all her teeth. She was put to death by stoning.

Theodota is commemorated by the Latin Church on September 29th.

CREED.

The text of the Creed which follows the story of Theodota will be found in my Introduction to *The Four Gospels in Syriac, transcribed from the Sinaitic Palimpsest*, by Robert L. Bensly, J. Rendel Harris, and F. Crawford Burkitt, pp. viii—xiv.

SUSANNA.

As the story of Susan belongs to the Old Testament Apocrypha, I intended giving only a collation of the Palimpsest text on that of Walton, in an Appendix. I did not begin to do this until after part of Cyprian and Justa was already in print; and I then discovered that the text of Susan represents quite an independent translation from the Greek; and that a collation would not only occupy more space than the story itself, but would be very troublesome to the reader. Therefore the tale is printed in full as Appendix I.

CYPRIAN AND JUSTA.

Eterno sera en el mundo
El majico Cipriano. CALDERON.

I have printed the text of the fifth century British Museum MS. Add. 12,142, giving that of the Syriac Palimpsest where this is deficient. The variants are from the Palimpsest, excepting where its text takes the place of honour, and there the variants are from Add. 14,645.

The peculiar interest of this story lies in the fact that it is the original form of a legend which, during the Middle Ages, rooted itself in popular superstition, and which has in later times blossomed again in the very highest walks of literature. Cyprian's demon, like the little Afrît of the *Arabian Nights' Entertainments*, has left his bottle, and has expanded under the fostering care of a Marlowe, a Calderon and a Goethe till he fills the world with his presence, and he is recognised wherever the "Geist der stets verneint," shows his ugly face. We are indebted to a paper by Mr Baring Gould in the *Contemporary Review* for 1877[1], and to the able work of

---

[1] Early Christian Greek Romances, *Contemporary Review*, Oct. 1877 (p. 864).

Dr Theodore Zahn, *Cyprian von Antiochien und die deutsche Faustsage* for our information about the origin of the legend.

Cyprian, Bishop of Carthage, was martyred on Sept. 17th A.D. 258. According to the martyrologies, a woman named Rosula suffered at the same time. Popular imagination seized on an admission which Cyprian had made to Donatus regarding his conduct before his conversion, and it exaggerated this into a confession that he had committed some heinous crime. The Greek romance of Cyprian and Justa, appearing about a century after his death, was an embodiment of those vague ideas which were current amongst the people.

St Gregory of Nazianzus, who died in A.D. 390, in his oration on the festival of St Cyprian of Carthage, adopts this romantic story. The historical Cyprian died on Sept. 14th, 16th or 17th and the fabulous one on Sept. 26th. The Anglican Reformers cut the real one out of the Calendar, and retained the fabulous one.

The Latin Church commemorates SS. Cyprian and Justina on Sept. 26th; but it does not confound the former with his great namesake.

The Greek Church commemorates them on Oct. 2nd, and a Cyprian and Juliana, who may possibly be the same, on Nov. 1st. Three later saints of the same name are remembered on March 10th, July 5th, and Aug. 17th but the real Cyprian appears to be quite overlooked. Some trace of his influence may be noticed, however, in the story of Cyprian and Justa, as related in the Συναξαριστής.

" He (Cyprian) was a native of Karchedon, or *Karthagena* in Libya, but he dwelt in Antioch of Syria, in the time of the Emperor Decius, in the year 250."

Here the real and the fictitious personages are evidently mingled, the former belonging to Carthage, the latter to Antioch.

A foot-note of the editor informs us that the body of the

great St Cyprian was hidden by a woman named Matrona or Rufina, a kinswoman of the Emperor Claudius.

Eudoxia, consort of Theodosius II., turned the legend into a metrical form, in imitation of the Homeric epics. She had done the same with the Octateuch, or first eight books of the Greek Bible, whilst spending her latter years in Jerusalem, A.D. 441—460, but these compositions are not of great literary value[1].

It is very interesting to observe how this simply told legend has been glorified by the genius of two modern dramatists, one a gifted representative of the Latin races; the other, possessing the very loftiest intellect of any purely Teutonic people.

Calderon's play is evidently moulded on the Christian legend. Its first acts are commonplace, being remarkable only for verbal quips and cranks; but with the sale of Cyprian's soul to the demon it rises to a higher plane, and occasionally touches a point of real sublimity.

It begins with the demon introducing himself to Cyprian— a lonely scholar who is vainly searching for some light on the nature of the true God, and on the question "Are there many gods, or only One?" It then passes to an impending duel between two young nobles, Lelio and Florio, who are rivals for the love of the beautiful Christian maiden, Justina. Cyprian pacifies them and averts the duel, by offering to call on the young lady and ascertain which of the two gallants she prefers. He does so, and is himself smitten by her beauty; whilst his two servants, Moscon and Clarin, fall madly in love with her maid Livia. Livia settles her own affair by agreeing to favour either swain on alternate days, but Justina refuses to hear a whisper of courtship from anyone. Her father Lisandro, is in great embarrassment, not only from his being deeply in debt, but because he apprehends a fresh persecution of the Christians. Cyprian, believing himself alone, bemoans aloud

---

[1] See Dr Rendel Harris' *Homeric Centones*, p. 36.

his hopeless love, and declares his readiness to give away his soul if by doing so he might gratify it. The voice of the demon replies: "Yo la azeto," "I accept it." Sounds of thunder and tempest, with flashes of fiery lightning, seal this pact, and the demon steps out of a black boat from a stormy sea in the guise of a sailor. He introduces himself as a learned scholar, and offers to teach Cyprian the art of magic, so that he may weave irresistible spells around his lady love, but on the condition of selling his soul. Cyprian accepts the offer, and signs the deed with his own blood.

The demon in the meantime has ruined the reputation of Justina by climbing down from her balcony, in the guise of a man, whilst Lelio and Florio are watching the house during the night. For a whole year Cyprian lives with the demon in a dark cave, and on the anniversary of the day when he signed the fatal compact, he emerges glorying in his own proficiency in magic, able as he phrases it, to give lessons to his master, and confident of being able to draw Justina into his meshes. Clarin, one of his servants, follows his example by signing away his soul in blood from the desire of possessing Livia. Evil spirits haunt Justina, and ghostly voices suggest to her that the greatest glory of this world is love. The demon urges her to seek Cyprian, and even uses force to draw her towards him, but when she exclaims "My defence is in God," he is obliged to release her. He then resorts to stratagem and produces a phantom, clad in Justina's robes. Cyprian, believing that she has come in answer to his call, lays siege to her, and is about to embrace her, when on removing her veil, he discovers that she is a skeleton. Frozen with horror, he hears voices saying "Thus, Cyprian, are all the glories of the world." He demands the blood-written schedule back from the demon, who refuses to give it up, on the plea that the undertaking had been fulfilled, for he had drawn Justina into Cyprian's arms. Cyprian obliges him reluctantly to confess who had protected the maiden, and to declare further that there is only one Almighty God, who is perfect goodness, and that this God is the God of the Christians. The demon then insists that Cyprian has become his slave and reveals his own personality. They engage in a struggle which threatens to become a mortal one for Cyprian, but as the demon is squeezing the breath out of him, he suddenly exclaims: "Great God of the Christians! I fly to Thee in my troubles," and he is at once released.

The Governor of Antioch then appears on the scene, and agrees to release Lelio, his own son, and Florio, who have been imprisoned for disorderly conduct. Then comes Cyprian, who is supposed to be mad, because he is proclaiming aloud his faith in the One Unseen God. The play ends with Cyprian and Justina mounting the scaffold together, Justina comforting her lover with the assurance of the Divine mercy. The actual execution is not seen; but as their bodies and severed heads are being shown to the populace, the demon springs upon the stage, and confesses aloud that he had calumniated Justina; that Cyprian had washed the schedule clean with his life-blood; that the two were now happy; and that he was forced by God to make the declaration. With this very stagey device the play ends.

The chief difference between this story and that of our legendary text is this: that in the former Cyprian is himself the lover of Justina; and in the latter he employs demons to allure her into the net of a client who asks for his intervention. Calderon's drama is certainly on a far higher plane of literary merit than is the legend; but the sublimity to which it rises is sadly spoiled by the lame device of the demon's confession.

Goethe has taken the story of Christopher Marlowe's Faust as the foundation of his own great drama, and he departs much more widely from the early Christian legend. Faust himself, as Dr Zahn has remarked, is the product of a society which had for centuries been permeated by Christian sentiment, and he seeks to penetrate the mysteries of Nature, of human Destiny, and of the Deity, by the aid of magic, before the arch demon Mephistopheles proffers his help.

Margaret is very unlike the pure, chaste and somewhat colourless conception of Justina, she is more human and appeals much more strongly to our sympathies. Margaret has one point in common with Calderon's hero and heroine ; we receive a hint of her escape from thraldom and of her actual salvation immediately after her appeal to God for protection. Faust and Gretchen do not die the death of martyrs ; but their life-story forms the framework of one of the most profoundly philosophical and charmingly natural of dramas.

Bedjan's text of Cyprian and Justina is from a manuscript in Berlin (Sachau No. 222).

The British Museum contains, besides the text which I have edited from Add. 12,142, some fragments of the story in Add. 14,629, Add. 12,174 and Add. 14,738.

The story of Cyprian and Justa, in Arabic and Greek, from Sinai MSS. will be found in No. VIII. of *Studia Sinaitica*.

SELECT NARRATIVES.

By the strength of our Lord Jesus Christ, the Son of _{f. 2 b} the Living God, I begin, I the sinner, John the Recluse of Beth-Mari Kaddisha, to write select narratives about the holy women, first the book of the Blessed Lady Thecla, disciple of Paul, the Blessed Apostle. My brethren, pray for me.

EUGENIA.

The Acts and the Martyrdom of the Blessed Eugenia _{f. 21 a} and of her father Philip and of all who were martyred with them.

Whilst Commodus was reigning, ruler of the transitory world, in the great and famous city of Rome, in his own seventh consulate, he gave the command of a province to Philip, one of his magnates, and sent him to Alexandria the great city, which is in the land of Egypt, and he thus gave him the command of all who were in the country, rich and poor, great and small, and of all the Roman troops who were there, that they should be obedient and _{f. 21 b} submissive to the laws and to the commandments which should be established and decreed to them by him. Now when Philip received the command of the province from the Emperor with his consort Claudia and his two sons, Avita and Sergius, and his daughter the virgin Eugenia, they travelled from Rome to Alexandria and arrived quickly. But immediately when they had entered that country he sent decrees through every city and province, and thus it was written in them. By the commandments of the victorious Emperors. All the Egyptians shall be governed by the laws of the Romans, and they shall live by their customs continually.

Now Eugenia the daughter of this Eparch Philip was about sixteen years old, and she was proficient in much wisdom and in the learning of the Greeks and the Romans, and she was very skilful in speech; so that the philosophers and the wise men were amazed at her wisdom and her discourse and at the erudition of her mind.

Now upon a certain day her father asked her, saying to her, Art thou willing, my daughter, that I should betroth thee to Aquilina the son of Hypatus? For behold! we know him that he is a wise and rich man and worthy of being thy betrothed.

f. 22 a

But she answered and said to her father: It is expedient that I should espouse him who loveth integrity, and purity, and holiness; rather than this man concerning whom thou hast told me that he hath transient riches and possessions. For far better is he who hath promised glorious things to the soul which is pure from evil, than the natural man who is mortal and transitory. For there had fallen into her hands the book of the story of the discipleship of Thecla the holy virgin, and of Paul the Apostle; and by it the eyes of her understanding were enlightened in the fear of God. For when she read in it she wept passionately in secret, continually, and sighed bitterly; and she was the more grieved because she was the daughter of people who were heathens and were without the knowledge of God. Now truly when she read in this story of the discipleship of Thecla the

f. 22 b

virgin, she was desirous in her soul, longing every day that she might be of the religion of the Christians, and continue in the doctrine and in the reading of their sacred books. And on a certain day she asked of her parents that they would grant this favour to her and allow her to go from the city to a certain village to amuse herself, and they consented and allowed her to go, because they loved her greatly.

Now there went with her many eunuchs and servants for her honour. Now as the litter in which she was sitting with the pomp of noble women was going along, Eugenia was reading within it in the book of Thecla, and was meditating on a passage in it. And she said to the two eunuchs who were with her, whose names were these, Proteus and Hyacinthus: Do not disregard what the poets in the error of their hearts imagine and say concerning God, and what things also the philosophers in the error of their hearts falsify and deny about God, who is God in truth f. 23a and verity. For is such truth perchance found amongst those who are called gods as that which is made known in these sacred books of theology about the true God and about His mighty power? But little to a degree, and very miserable and childish is a soul which calls stones and bits of carved wood, blind and deaf and without feeling, gods, and calls them to its help.

Now as the Blessed Eugenia said these things for the salvation of these her two eunuchs, the three of them began to consider together amongst themselves, discussing and investigating concerning the true God and concerning the worship of His Divinity. And they said to each other: There is nothing more important than this, that a man should fear the true God, and should be a worshipper and honourer of Him alone, in his faith and in his love and in his good works. Now when they had talked about these things and things like them with each other, as if in answer

they heard the Christians who were singing and saying:
All the gods of the nations are demons; but the Lord made
the heavens.

When the Blessed Eugenia heard these things, she
commanded that her litter should be instantly detained
and should stand still. For the fear of the Christ entered
into her heart when she heard this singing and she answered
and said to the two eunuchs who were with her: We have
quickly found evidence concerning the truth which the sacred
books speak about concerning the true power of God who
is to be worshipped, and about the perdition and vanity
of the polluted worship of idols. But now we have learned
the truth about both religions. What therefore shall we do
that we may approach that glorious wisdom, and by means
of a better life may be able to attain to these mysteries
of the Divinity? Let us henceforth look to ourselves,
my brethren. For how long shall we occupy ourselves
with these useless things of error? Let us cast from
ourselves all these vanities of this world, and instead
of them let us meditate on the living words of God, and on

saving faith. Let our minds be established, that by these
things we may be able to flee and escape from the snares
of Satan and from the net of the adversary, and that we
may hold and may be established in the faith of the Christ
the Saviour of the souls of men.

And again the Blessed One answered and said to
Proteus and to Hyacinthus: The fashion of this transient
world has appointed me your mistress; but now the fear
of God, which is implanted in our hearts by His love,
makes me your sister, and henceforth, my brethren, I
counsel you that we be one soul in the faith of God,
in one love of God, despising and rejecting all the honours
and desires and luxuries of this world, and progressing
in love and in faith, and coming near to the glories of

the world that passeth not away for ever; having nothing opposed to us to hinder us by its hateful counsels that we should henceforth be removed from all this blessedness which meets us by the grace of God and by our good will.

And now as I speak to you and instruct you, so do. f. 24 b Remove in the first place the hair from my head, and all this ornament that is upon me, and take away your own afterwards, and let us change our dress and direct the course of our journey this night to believing people, the servants of the living God. Let the two of you holding me on my right hand and on my left, gently with secrecy let me down from this litter without anyone perceiving it; and let the litter be going on empty, and let those who are with it be imagining that I am sitting inside it, and we three all alike in man's clothing will go joyfully to the people of God.

Now the counsel of the Blessed One pleased these eunuchs, and the next day they did joyfully as she had said to them. Now the Christ in whom they fully believed sent immediately in a very little while His grace to them. For as soon as she descended from her litter, and they f. 25 a began to travel and to go on the road, the saint of God, the bishop Helenus, happened to be accompanying them with a great multitude who were with him, praising and singing and saying together: The paths of the righteous are straight, and the paths of the holy are ordered.

Then said the Blessed Eugenia to Proteus and to Hya-cinthus: Do ye understand the force of these words that they are singing now? Do ye know that upon us is accomplished the meaning of the words which we are hearing now from the Christians who are singing and praising their God; those which we also were speaking to each other yesterday concerning the truth of God, and concerning His mighty power? For we heard before

holy men singing and praising God and saying that all
the gods of the nations are demons, and we removed
ourselves far from the ruinous worship of idols: and now

again lo! we hear thousands of men singing together
and saying: The paths of the righteous are straight and
the ways of the just are equal.   Now since we have heard
these sacred words, let us go in with a good will and mingle
with this crowd of singers, and let us be of them and be
numbered in their ranks, that we may enter with them into
the life that passeth not away, although we have been
called late, as if at eventide, to the knowledge of the truth.

Now when they had entered and mingled with the
crowd of Christians, they asked some of them, saying:
Who is that old man who is sitting by himself in the midst
of the people in a high place as if in honour?   But some
of the crowd answered and said unto them: That is the
bishop Helenus, who has been educated from his birth in
a monastery of Christian people, he who by his acceptable
prayers was saved from the midst of a burning fire; and

what is to be told concerning the beauty and excellence of his former deeds!   For lo! a short time ago a
certain wizard who dwelt here, whose name was Iraus,
approached the people of the Christians with the wicked
artifice of his magic, and desired to turn away their minds
from the sacred writings of theology, and from the certain
hope which is signified in their living words.   He waxed
bold in his wickedness and approached the bishop Helenus
and began to speak to him vain words and of the corruption
of his error.   But when the holy man saw the impudence
of his wicked words, and knew that he could not reply
to him about the truth in words, he said with a loud voice
in the presence of all the people who were assembled there:
Why need we argue in words with the son of perdition
who now disturbs us?   For behold! he is not willing to

submit to our own words nor to our teaching that he may
turn to the truth. For by the seductiveness and incitement
of his words he has caused many to fall from the faith of f. 26 b
God wherein they were standing. And behold! down to
the present time he is eager in his wickedness that he
may subvert and throw down those who are established
and confirmed in their faith from the hope of their God.
But henceforth in the first place it is incumbent on us to
show by an experiment and by a deed that it is God who
guides and helps all those who believe in Him and rely
upon Him. He who by the hands of me, His humble
and weak servant, is ready to show the glorious power
of His sovereignty and the sublime redemption which He
works for all His servants who love Him with their whole
heart in truth and in verity.

And when the holy one, bishop Helenus, had said these
things, he said again to all the people who were standing
there and listening to them: Kindle a great fire in the
midst of the city; and let us enter it together, I and this
son of perdition who is leading you astray, and let us
stand in the midst of the flame. And the one of us whom
his God shall rescue from the fire and who does not burn, f. 27 a
his religion is true, and his God is the true God and
is able to save from the fire all those who trust in Him.
And when the bishop Helenus had said these things, this
counsel pleased all the people; they said to him: Thou
hast well said. Now when they had kindled a great
fire, the holy bishop Helenus commanded that they both
should go in together without fear, and that they should
stand in the midst of the flame. But the wizard answered
and said: Let it not be thus; but let us enter each of us
alone. Now go thou in first, because thou hast counselled
and incited the people that this should happen. And
immediately, swiftly, the Blessed Helenus, with great con-

fidence in God his helper, spread out his hands towards
heaven, and with sobs and with many tears called to God
in his prayers, saying: Thou knowest, our Lord Jesus the
Christ, Son of the Living God, the readiness of my soul;

f. 27 b   Thou wert the fourth who didst appear to the three children
of the house of Hanania in the midst of the furnace of fire.
Thou knowest, my Lord and my God, that I had not one
wish for human glory; but all my labour and longing and
the eagerness of my soul is for the redemption of Thy
people, over whom in Thy grace Thou hast appointed me a
shepherd, whom the enemy and hater of good by means of
his minister hath plotted to turn from the plain path of life.
And because of this, for the redemption of Thy people I go
joyfully into this fire, for there I shall find Thee before
me. But sprinkle upon me swiftly the dew of Thy mercy,
so that this fire may not at all touch me. And when he had
said these things in his prayers, he signed himself with the
sign of the cross and entered, and stood confidently exulting
in the midst of the flame of the fire a long time, whilst in
nothing was he hurt by that fire. Then when the people
who were assembled there saw this great miracle which had

f. 28 a   happened they laid hold of Iraus the wizard and without
his consent threw him into the fire. But when he began to
burn the blessed bishop Helenus ran and seized him by his
hand so that he might rescue him. For although he was
justly tortured in that fire, as his impudence deserved, yet
the bishop Helenus seized and brought him out of it alive.

But when all the people had insulted that wizard and
stoned him with stones, they left him and went away from
there.

But him whom ye see, the grace of God has magnified
him whilst continually without ceasing he praises and
glorifies and exalts God, who by His hand hath wrought
redemption for His people.

Then the blessed Eugenia with those two eunuchs who were with her, Proteus and Hyacinthus, fell down before the holy bishop Helenus and did obeisance to him. And they implored and besought him to confirm them in the faith of the Christ; and they opened their mouths and persuaded him and besought him that by his hand they might approach to the knowledge of God completely. f. 28 b The blessed one answered and said to them, My children, be ye continually in the church of God, and be ye zealous at all times in the holy service of your Lord, and thus the great day of the revelation of His coming shall find you watching and ready.

But the blessed Eugenia besought him and said unto him, I beseech of thee, my Lord, pray for me, and commend me to God, He whom thou servest gloriously from thy youth. For we three, my Lord, are by family Romans, and children of those who worship idols. But the mercy of thy Lord and His grace hath called us. When we heard His voice we did not delay to follow it, but immediately swiftly we left the vain worship of idols. And as we were seeking to journey after the sacred footsteps of thy holiness the grace of God brought us hither. And when the blessed ones had related these things to the holy Helenus he was silent and did not speak to them, for all the things that f. 29 a had been related to him had been revealed to him by the revelation of the Holy Spirit. And because it was evening they knelt and received a blessing from him, and thus they departed from his presence. But on the following day they came to the church and desired to appear to the blessed bishop. But a certain priest who dwelt with him chanced to be there; an illustrious and excellent man, whose name was Eutropius. And they persuaded him to go in and remind the bishop about them. And he went in to him with eagerness and said to him: Three young men,

brethren, have come here of those who have forsaken the
fear and the worship of idols, and they desire to become
servants of the Christ, and to be numbered amongst His
people, and to be amongst those who believe in Him
and are admitted to His glorious mysteries. And they
desire so great a gift by the hand of thy holiness and long
to be worthy. Then said the blessed Helenus, I praise
Thee, our Lord Jesus the Christ, that Thou hast caused us
to attain to all this, and by Thy grace hast deemed us

f. 29 b   to be worthy. I will see those of whom Thou hast already
told me by the revelation of the Holy Spirit. And he
commanded and they entered his presence, and he rose
immediately and prayed. And when he had finished his
prayer, he took hold of the hand of Eugenia with those two
who were with her, and said to them, How have ye received
the knowledge of the truth, and committed yourselves to
God, and [how] did ye ask to see me His humble servant?
What have ye heard about me that ye have come to me?
Reveal it to me, for I wish to know it from you, and I
seek to see the good fruits of your promptitude, if it be
that you wish to approach God with all your mind.

And the blessed Eugenia answered and said to him:
We have considered amongst ourselves that it is not fitting
that we should name the adorable name of God on stones
and wooden things without feeling. And whilst we were
discussing amongst ourselves which is the true religion in
which the most high and adorable God delights, the grace
of our Lord brought us hither. For we heard some of

f. 30 a   you who were singing together and saying that all the
gods of the nations are demons, but the Lord made the
heavens. And when we heard this blessed voice, we dismissed immediately and swiftly the religion of idols from
us. And we forsook their worship in haste. And we came
hither eagerly, and we journeyed with all the people of the

believers in thy footsteps[1], Father, whilst we were believing
in God who will help us, that we may assent to thy faith,
and be established in thy truth, and we may show by deeds
the truth of the words which have been spoken by us to
thy holiness. But we three are all of us brothers. One
of us is named Proteus, and another Hyacinthus, and I am
called Eugenius. And in reply to these things which
bishop Helenus heard from Eugenia, he answered and said
to her, Thou art well called Eugenius; because joyfully
and heroically thou doest everything, and thy soul is
perfected ; and thou approachest joyfully to the contest of
Christ. But know that God has revealed and made known
to us that thou art called Eugenia, and whence thou art f. 30 b
come and whose daughter thou art; and who these two
are who have come hither with thee, our Lord hath shewn
it clearly to me ; and by the good will that was in thee
towards God also those ones are found perfect, and as-
senters to thy faith. And he commanded them that they
should be constantly three months in the churches and in
the monasteries, that they might be helped by the sight
and by the speech of many, and be established completely
in the faith of God. And then afterwards he made them
approach the baptism of atonement and made them partakers of the glorious mysteries of the Divinity. Now
when he had done all these excellent things to them he
led them and brought them into a monastery of men
and committed them to the Abbot, and commanded him
concerning them that he should have a care over them.
But their deeds he revealed to no one as yet.

But at the first time of the discipleship of the blessed
ones when Proteus and Hyacinthus had let down the
blessed Eugenia from her litter, the litter went on empty, f. 31 a
whilst the young men who were going before it and behind

---

[1] Literally in the footsteps of thy Paternity.

it knew nothing about what had happened; for they supposed that she was sitting in it and going. But the
household of the blessed Eugenia when they thought that
she had arrived from the village whither she had gone,
went out to meet her with joy and to welcome her with
exultation. But when they did not find her as they had
expected, they lifted up their voice with weeping and with
bitter wailing.

And they enquired of those who were with her what
had become of Eugenia. They excused themselves, Until
we arrived here we did not know what had happened,
but we were trusting that she was sitting in the inside of
this litter. And after these things there was a tumult and
a great uproar in all the cities and in that country. And
every one was in distress and in great grief because of her.
And she was sought for in every place and was not found.
f. 31 b   For her parents were mourning for their daughter; and
her brothers for their sister; and her servants for their
mistress. And every citizen was plunged into great
sorrow, because they saw in what a grief her parents and
her household were because of her. And they went
round about in all the places and provinces seeking for
Eugenia.

Now they inquired of the country people who were in
that place and of the women who practised necromancy and
they offered sacrifices to the idols on her behalf. And when
they had sought for her in every place and she was not
found, all the deluded people, the worshippers of idols, said
this concerning her, The immortal gods have snatched her
away, and she is exalted to heaven and she mingles with
them. And when her father heard these things from the
impostors he believed them, and his great grief and sore
sorrow turned to much consolation. And they made her
a statue of pure gold, and set it up in the city. But her

mother Claudia, and her brothers Avita and Sergius found
no way whatever of being consoled in their grief.

Now the blessed Eugenia in the dress of a man with
Proteus and Hyacinthus, in one perfect love, were in the f. 32 a
monastery which we have already named progressing in
the fear of God every day, so that in a short time they
were repeating by heart all the Holy Scriptures.   But
while the blessed ones were occupied with these chaste
and holy deeds three years afterwards the Abbot of that
monastery in which Eugenia with her two eunuchs was, fell
on sleep, and his soul went to his Lord in peace.

And some time after the death of this Abbot it pleased
all the brethren of this monastery to appoint Eugenia
Abbot over them.   But the blessed Eugenia declined this,
for her conscience admonished her that she was a woman,
and it was not fitting that she should be commander [and]
governor to the men of God.   And moreover she was
afraid lest she might cause the minds of the brethren to
stumble who were advising and persuading her to do this ;
for she saw clearly that the minds of all of them were
consenting to that idea.   And the blessed Eugenia answered
and said to them, Many a time ye have heard such words f. 32 b
in your own synod, for ye say that our Lord Jesus the
Christ will reveal and make known to us such things as be
profitable according to His will.   And now, if ye command
it, let the holy Gospel be brought into [our] midst and let
us stand and pray with fervour, and let us beseech the
Lord that He will reveal and show to us such things as
be profitable ; and let us afterwards open and read, and
whatsoever be the first passage that is found, let us assent
to it, and let us hear it and do as it commands us.

Now when the holy Gospel came and was placed in the
midst, they all stood and prayed.   And afterwards the
blessed Eugenia took it in her two hands and kissed it and

pressed it upon her eyes. And she worshipped the Lord
and opened it. And when they saw what she had done
there was great quiet amongst them. And when she had
opened it, she found the place in which it is written that
our Lord said to his disciples, Ye know that the chiefs of
the nations are their lords, and their great men rule over
them. It shall not be so among you, but whosoever among

f. 33 a   you wishes to be the chief, let him be the servant and
minister of every man. Now after this reading Eugenia
said to them, Since ye have made known that this is your
wish, it is incumbent upon us that we fulfil the commandments of the Christ. For it is required of a servant that
he be obedient to his fellows in the fear of the Christ
whilst he is cautious in his mind and in his estimation of
himself; blameless and faultless let him draw near joyfully
to God. When they had all assented to the words which
the blessed Eugenia spoke to them, in order that she might
not resist and vex them she accepted for herself only the
title of Abbot. But they entreated her and besought her
that she would accept all the rule of the monastery, as
head and governor. She yielded to them also in this
behaving amongst them with all humility and showing
indeed the fruits of this humility. And the things which
the last ought to do to the first in the service of the saints,
she in her eagerness and in her humility used to do, all the

f. 33 b   service pertaining to the fraternity ; for she drew water
from the well and cut wood and swept all the rooms of the
convent, and fulfilled all the service of the brethren. And
she made a little cell for herself by the side of the door of
the monastery that she might be continually in it, that she
might not be a burden on the brothers who were with her,
and be better off in her dwelling than all those who were
with her. For at the time of the service she would enter
first and all the brethren would find her there. And there

was not in all that fraternity any one who excelled her in humility, and at all times she was assiduous with the brethren, warning and teaching them that they should not use any oaths at all, but that the truth should be spoken amongst them with quiet speech. For we learn from the commandments of God that we should conduct ourselves with all propriety and holiness and humility and patience. And let us have this eagerness continually, that God may in nothing be despised by us through the transgression of His commandments. For he hath denied his Lord, who teaches his companions that they should do things which f. 34 a his Lord hath not commanded to be done. Now whilst they were learning these commandments every day from her, the brethren who were with her were the more confirmed in their faith and in their love and in good works. For neither by day nor by night did she cease from prayer and from the reading of the Scriptures. Now whilst she was living such a life, there was given to her by means of the grace of God the gift of healing, so that she cast out demons from men by means of the sign of the cross of our Lord, and health was given from God by her hands to those who were sick and afflicted. But because our word is not sufficient to describe the excellency of each one of her first works, such as they were, we leave them and we come briefly to relate her chaste and holy deeds.

Now the wife of a certain senator who was very rich in goods and in much wealth, whose name was Melania, had been sick of a fever and of an ague for a long time. She heard about the blessed Eugenia, that our Lord wrought f. 34 b healing by her hand to those who were afflicted; and she sent for her. And the blessed Eugenia did not decline to go at once with those who came for her. And when she entered her presence and saw her, she immediately signed

the sign of the cross on the breast and betwixt the eyes of
Melania and prayed. And immediately her fever fled from
her with her ague, and she was quickly made whole from
her sickness.

And immediately the blessed Eugenia returned swiftly
to her monastery. But after these things that had happened
Melania was sending continually to the blessed Eugenia
and bringing her to her [self] not knowing that she was a
woman. Now Eugenia went to her in the sincerity of her
heart and in the uprightness of her soul. But Melania
was not sending and fetching her with a sincere mind, nor
yet as believing that by her prayers she had been healed
of her sickness. But as she supposed that she was a man
she spoke unseemly words to her, for she said, "Why dost
thou trouble and vex thyself uselessly with fasting, and
spoilest the appearance of thy youth? Does God perchance
love sad people, and those whose faces are miserable; or
is He pleased with those who make their bodies lean with
hunger? Or is He glorified in those who flee from the
marriage-bed? Nor does He magnify those who crucify
themselves more than their companions. Does He command every man that he should accomplish the period of
his life without joy and comfort? Let us then draw nigh
and make use of the good things of this world which
are given to us by God, that we may not be like
ungrateful people and like people who are unworthy of
His gifts that are beside us. Believe henceforth to thy
advantage and thy profit in those things which are
spoken to thee by me. For when thou shalt be with me
in one love, thou shalt be heir of all that I possess. And
good times of enjoyment and of gladness shall pass over
thee. And thou shalt be lord of all my possessions. Also
of myself who am speaking to thee, and am persuading
thee. For I am adorned with beauty and with loveliness

f. 35 a

f. 35 b

and with gladness, and I have endless riches. And I consider that this is not wickedness; and it is not sin before God, if thou wilt be my husband. And when thou shalt cast away from thee this mind in which thou hast been stedfast for many years thou shalt enjoy good things."

But when Melania had said these things and more than these in her madness and her magical art, the Blessed Eugenia rose up in much agitation, and withstood the words of perdition and of death with which Melania was clothed, and she wished to free the soul of the latter from corruption. And she tried to persuade her and said: The desires of this world are destroyers of the souls of men. And wherein a man thinks that he seizes for a little while the transitory desires of this world, he robs himself of the enjoyment which passes not away for all eternity. Therefore let us not seek bodily desires at all, because Satan our enemy endeavours by them to sink and destroy the souls of men. When these words were f. 36 a spoken passionately by Eugenia, Melania shut her ear that she might not receive what was spoken to her. For her thoughts were bound with strong fetters of shameful desires. As it is written, to a guilty soul wisdom entereth not.

But Eugenia endeavoured and made a struggle that she might turn her if possible from the death of perdition towards salvation. And when she found no means of doing this, she departed from her, grieving about the destruction of her soul. But the mad Melania made herself sick and sent intercessors and persuaders to the Blessed Eugenia, so that she might come and see her and pray over her and she might be healed. And she went into her presence with confidence, and sat down beside her in an inner apartment. And she took hold of Eugenia without shame and wished to embrace her secretly. And she

f. 36 b   spoke to her unchaste and infamous words in her wickedness.

Then the Blessed Eugenia perceiving the treachery of
Satan and the cunning of the mad woman his servant,
stretched out her right hand and signed herself with the
sign of the cross, and with weeping and with sobs said
in a loud voice, Justly wert thou called Melania, for a
heavy blackness and a putrid filth wells up within thee.
Righteously art thou called Melania. For thou art the
daughter of nameless sin and a guide to perdition to
those who shall perish through thee, a daughter of everlasting Gehenna ; a troubled spring of putridity, a fountain
running with shame and overflowing, the enemy of God
and the abode of the Evil one. For there is not even one
good thing in thy heart, because thou art the dwelling-
place of Satan. And thou art not worthy to have part
or company with the servants of God.

Now when Melania had heard this contumely, she
f. 37 a   flamed into a great rage not enduring the shame that was
hers. For she reflected that perhaps this rumour would
come to the hearing of men, and she would become a
reproach and a derision in the eyes of all her acquaint-
ances. And she went at once to Alexandria, and publicly
in the sight of all the people she approached the governor
of the city, and made an accusation before him against the
Blessed Eugenia and said : I denounce a certain young
madman who has been saying of himself that he is a
Christian. I sent for him and fetched him, that he might
cure me ; because I had been told about him that he
could cure those who were pained and afflicted, and heal
them of their sicknesses. And when I had commanded
that he should enter my presence he immediately began to
speak shameful and vile words and would have led me
into disgrace. And why is it necessary for me to say

more? For at last he wished in his madness to assault me like a slave, and if a certain girl had not happened to be with me in my chamber, by whose help I escaped from f. 37 b his hands and he prevailed not against me, he would otherwise, as his lasciviousness inclined, have wrought his pleasure on me.

Now when the governor had heard this accusation, he was greatly troubled. And he sent a troop of soldiers and commanded that she and all who were with her should be bound in iron fetters, and they should come speedily and their cause should be heard before all the people; and afterwards they should be cast to the wild beasts. But when the day arrived on which it was decreed concerning them, that the examination of the Blessed Eugenia and of all those who were with her should take place, having put iron fetters on all their limbs and having bound them tight, they brought them in and made them stand up in the court in the sight of all the people. And when the crowd of people who had come together on their account saw them, not knowing the truth of what had happened, they lifted up their voice together and cried out against them, but those who were on the side of the mad Melania were shouting the more, and some of them were f. 38 a crying that they should be cast into the fire, and be put to death in it, and their lives should perish, others were crying out that they should be food for the wild beasts. And others said that they should be punished with severe and bitter punishments, as was befitting their impudence. For with one consent the mind of all the people was against them, as against people who had done something worthy of death. Then the governor commanded that the clamour of the people should cease; and when they were quiet from what they were excited about, they brought in the Blessed Eugenia and set her in the court

before the governor openly in the sight of all the people.
And he began to question her, saying : What confidence
induced thee to approach the patrician lady Melania for the
purpose of offering her this wicked outrage ? Thou didst
enter in the deceitful dress of the Christians, and as one
skilful in the craft of healing, that thou mightest bring a

f. 38 b   woman of the aristocracy to the shame of wantonness.
Did the Christ perhaps teach you to do things like these ?
And is this the profession of your religion, that ye should
do deeds of corruption and uncleanness ?

But the Blessed Eugenia returned an answer with much
courage to the governor saying : I was praying that I
might overcome all the temptations which should come
on me into my mind and conquer them.   And that I
might reserve this accusation of calumny and oppression
for the judgment that is to be.   But in order that the
purity of truth may not be abashed by those who out of
an evil mind unjustly attack it ; for purity which is guided
by modesty cannot at all be hidden, for it will bring not
merely the praise of men to those who love it, but it will
be impelled to exist for the honour of God who gave it.
For chastity and holiness and . modesty are preserved
completely by wise men, and the soul of the Christian
perfects all her works faithfully in the love of God.   I

f. 39 a   declare this my mind publicly in the midst of and in the
sight of all men.   For by nature I am a woman.   And I
was not able to fulfil the desire of my soul regarding the
fear of God, unless I changed myself into this chaste and
honourable and excellent guise.   And being a woman
by nature, in order that I might gain everlasting life, I
became a man for a short time, being emulous and imitating
my teacher Thecla : she who despised and rejected the
desires of this world, and became worthy of the good things
of heaven by means of her chastity and her life.   Therefore

I praised, Oh governor, every man who longs for the good
things that are with God, and him who because of the love
of the Christ hungers for so great excellence, and for the
weakness which imitates the strength of full grown men.
And because of this I also by the impulse of the love of
God and by the fear of His sovereignty took the dress
of an adult man in private and in public, keeping my
virginity spotless to the Christ my Lord.   f. 39 b

And when she had said these things, she rent the
garment which she wore from the top as far as her girdle,
and that which was hidden from the sight of men was
instantly revealed, and the chaste breasts which were upon
the bosom of a pure virgin were seen.   And when she had
done this, and convinced every one what she was, she
at once swiftly covered and wrapped herself up with
the rags which she had torn.   And she continued and
said to the governor: Thou art my own bodily father, and
ye are my brothers Avita and Sergius.   For I am thy
daughter Eugenia, she who because of the love of Christ
rejected this world and its desires with my two eunuchs
Proteus and Hyacinthus who came with me to the covenant
of the Christ, my Lord.   And my Saviour Jesus the Christ
has abundantly presented Himself to thee, that when I
shall be to thee a teacher, the desire of the victory of the f. 40 a
Christ, him in whom I believe and hope that he will keep
me in purity until the end, may in the presence of every
one come upon thee.

Then the father recognized his daughter, and the
brothers their sister.   And they ran before all the people
and embraced her, and kissed her weeping.   This was also
made known to her mother Claudia.   And she ran in
haste with her maid-servants to the theatre, and she also
entered and wept before all the people, and embraced and
kissed her weeping bitterly.   And they brought costly

robes and clothed her against her will. And in order
that she might be seen by all men they lifted her and
placed her on a high place. And all the people when
they saw her shouted with a loud voice saying, One is our
Lord, Jesus the Christ, the true God of the Christians.

Now the Bishops, and the priests, and the deacons, and
all the people of the Christians were sitting outside the
theatre watching that when the saints should be put to

f. 40 b   death they might take their corpses, and bury them.
They also went into the theatre praising and blessing God
and saying, "Thy right hand, O Lord! hath done mighty
things; Thy right hand, O Lord! hath broken thine enemies.
Now that the Blessed one hath been exalted above all
men it has happened by the providence of God that by
her modesty and by her dignity all who behold her might
be helped. And that the glory of such modesty should
not be concealed, all men seeing it, fire fell from heaven
and burnt up Melania and all her house, and all that
belonged to her. And there was great joy among all the
people, and the church that had been closed eight years
before was opened. And every one believed in the Christ,
and became a Christian. And the Eparch was baptized,
and his sons Avitus and Sergius. And Claudia, the
mother of the Blessed Eugenia, was baptized also, with
all her hand-maidens; and people of the heathen without
number were turned to God.

f. 41 a   And the Christians recovered their privileges and were
singing praises as of old with their former customs, and all
Alexandria was like one church, and the presbyters only
were governing and serving the church. For he who
previously had been called of God as by the law and
had been bishop, had died in the Lord. Then all the
churches came together to Philip the Governor that he
might be bishop over them. And when he became (bishop)

by the grace of God which had called him, the holy
Church held him in great honour. But though he was
deemed worthy of this excellent degree of the Episcopacy,
he also governed the affairs of the city, because that until
now he held the command of the province. For he who
should remove him from the command of the province
had not yet arrived from the Emperors.

And at length all the inhabitants of Egypt were f. 41 b
converted by this means to the truth of the Christ from
the religion of idols; and the churches in all the cities and
villages which eight years before had been shut by the
heathen the persecutors of the truth, were opened; and
every day Christianity flourished and increased.

And whilst all these reformations were taking place by
the grace of the Christ, in all the churches of that country,
Satan, the persecutor of good things and teacher of hateful
things, and secret conspirer of evil things, awakened some
heathens amongst the chief men of the city, and incited
them to make it known to the Emperors, the Rulers of that
time, and these erring heathen did everything with envy
against the church of God and against the holy bishop
Philip. And there was sent against the blessed bishop
Philip a man who should depose him from the command of
the province, whose name was Perinus, for the Emperors
had given him power, that if what they had heard against
Philip from the chief men of Alexandria, were true, when
he should reach him he should immediately slay him f. 42 a
with the sword. Then Perinus arrived and entered the
city with much pomp and pride. But he was not able
to effect at once what had been commanded by the
Emperors against Philip, because all the people of the
city loved him greatly, and held him in great honour as
a good shepherd and a diligent governor. Now when
Perinus saw that he was not able to kill him publicly,

he sent with guile against him wicked and rascally men who were dressed in the honourable fashion of the Christians. And when they had entered his presence in the church, ,they found the Blessed one standing in fervent prayer before God. And when they approached him, that they might receive a blessing, they immediately struck him and killed him, as Zacharia was slain between the temple and the altar. He was in the office of a bishop one year and three months. And as he died in the confession and witnessing for the Christ, he went to his Lord in peace.

f. 42 b

But the Blessed Eugenia took up the body of her martyr-father, and wrapped it up carefully, and placed it by the side of the hostel which had been made by her mother Claudia for the comfort of strangers and afflicted people, close to a place which was called Natira[1]. And by the solicitude of her brothers Avitus and Sergius, a regal martyr-shrine was built upon it to the glory of the Christ, and for the help and edification of the souls of men. And when all these things were effectually finished, the blessed Eugenia with her mother Claudia and her brothers Avitus and Sergius went up from Alexandria to Rome, the grace of God accompanying them, through which they found favour before all the senate. And they were greatly welcomed by all men, so that one of them became proconsul in Carthage a city of Africa, and the other was appointed with honour over the country of Africa.

f. 43 a

But Claudia and Eugenia her daughter by the commandment of God were occupied every day with good works and chaste deeds which are pleasing to God. And they were turning many souls from the fear of idols and were bringing them near to God. And they were praised

---

[1] Perhaps "Nitria."

by all the noble women of senatorial rank and by all the virgins amongst the chiefs, and they were all zealous to imitate their life in the fear of the Christ.

But a certain virgin named Basilia, near of kin to the Emperor Gallienus, who was very prudent and wise, came secretly to the blessed Eugenia, and heard from her the word of truth. And immediately she was rooted in love in the depth of her understanding, and she believed fully in the Christ, so that no man was able from that time to uproot from within her heart the plant of faith in God. But because Basilia could not continually be seeing Eugenia, Eugenia gave Proteus and Hyacinthus her f. 43 b two eunuchs as a present to Basilia the virgin : and from that time, by day and by night, she was constant in the praise of God and in prayers and in reading of the sacred books.

Then the bishop of the city, whose name was Soter, a pure and holy man, who was very eminent in the fear of God and in the training of the teaching of the sacred books of theology, came to Basilia, and baptized her in the holy font, for the pardon of trespasses and for the remission of sins, and from the sacred books of theology he confirmed the minds of all who were with her in the faith of the Christ, so that they all together were prepared to go forward and to become willing martyrs. All the time that Bishop Soter presided over the church, the Christians were in tranquility and peace, for not one vexation was aroused against them by the enemies. But Bishop Cyprian in the city of Carthage endured many sufferings and afflictions because of the faith of God. For f. 44 a Maximus the Pro-consul by command of the Emperors who ordered him by means of letters, slew the holy Bishop Cyprian. Then Bishop Soter when he heard these things hid himself, and lived alone, but he taught many of the Roman citizens, honourable men, secretly. Now on a

certain day Basilia came to the blessed Eugenia, and
when she saw her she received her with great joy. And
Eugenia answered and said to her, This day our Lord
has made known to me clearly that from thy face which
is like a rose much blood will be shed. Now this means
that thou shalt have contended and conquered in the
confession of the Christ, thou shalt receive from Him the
crown of victory of thy martyrdom with joy.

Now when the blessed Basilia had heard these things
from the holy Eugenia, she lifted up her hands to heaven
and praised God with great joy. Now when they had
prayed and finishèd their prayer, they sat down, and
Basilia said to Eugenia, " To both of us as I see, our
Lord and our Redeemer Jesus the Christ has revealed
and shown us the glory of our crowns. For as thou
hast seen regarding me, so also to me the Christ has
already made known the time of thy departure. For I
saw that thou didst receive two crowns from heaven, one
because of the struggle for thy virginity which thou hast
made, and hast kept it spotless to the Christ ; and the
other one because thou shalt struggle in the conflict,
and shalt conquer the enemy, and thy blood will be shed
because of the Christ. These things thou art about to
receive."

Now when the blessed Eugenia had heard these things,
she rejoiced and exulted greatly, and called all the virgins
who had been drawn to the fear of God by her means and
who longed to preserve their virginity pure to the Christ,
and persuaded them that they should pray with her, and
commit her in their prayer to God. And after they had
finished their prayer, she began to talk with them, saying
to them : Now the time of vintage has arrived in which the
first-fruits are to be gathered, about which our Lord Jesus
the Christ hath made known to me by means of the mysteries

f. 44 b

f. 45 a

which He hath revealed to us beforehand. And now,
my beloved ones and my disciples, send ye me in the
first place before you to our Lord. And be ye also
watching and making ready that ye may go out to meet
the Christ, your betrothed, whilst your lamps are shining.
For the beauty of virginity appears first of all before God,
for it is the likeness of the angels which are in heaven.
And it is near to God the Almighty, and it is akin to the
life that is about to be revealed, and the mother of modesty
and the teacher of purity. And a mistress[1] without care,
and the height of happiness, and zealous for chastity, and
the illustrious crown of faith, the hope and succour and
honour of those who love it; the glory of the soul, and
eternal rest, the cause of good things and the guide to the
kingdom of heaven. Let there be for you no other labour
and urgency like this, that you may keep your virginity
purely and holily to the Christ the Son of God your
betrothed. For there are in this world incitements and
wicked desires, which remain for a short time with their f. 45 b
lovers, and afterwards beget weeping and sobbings in the
Gehenna of fire. These in their beginnings appear exhila-
rating to men, but in the end they torture those who do
them with bitter punishments and sore torments which are
endless. For they do their deeds without care in this
transitory world that they may be condemned completely
in everlasting endless torture. And now, my daughters,
honoured virgins, who bravely and believingly keep your
virginity along with me, remain in the love of each
other and in the love of God in which ye dwell and in
which ye are abundantly confirmed. For it is time now
that ye mourn and cry to God because of the former time
which has passed away, when error had fast hold of
you, that ye may be filled with everlasting joy, before

---

[1] Or "Martha."

the face of God Almighty. But I have committed you
to the Holy Spirit of God, whilst I believe and it is
certain to me that He will receive you in His kingdom
f. 46 a   spotless and blameless. Therefore do not seek for my
bodily appearance but let each of the beautiful examples
that I have shown you in my day be continually before
your face. And remember my teaching, humble though I
be, and love it every day.

When she had taught these things and things like them
and had committed them (to God) she kissed them all with
a holy kiss weeping. After she had saluted them, she
said : Be ye sound and true in our Lord, my daughters
and my sisters, for Basilia and Eugenia your sisters are
departing from this world to our Lord. But at that time,
one of the maidens of Basilia went to Pompeius her
betrothed and said to him, Dost thou know that thy
betrothed, the Lady Basilia, has been persuaded by
Eugenia to decline to be thy wife? And when Pompeius
heard these things from that girl, he was greatly troubled
and angry at Eugenia, and was sore distressed because
of Basilia his betrothed. And he went to her and wished
to enter the chamber where Basilia and Proteus and
Hyacinthus were performing their customary prayers and
f. 46 b   praises. He found the doors closed and he knocked at
the door and wished to enter their presence. But the
blessed Basilia sent to him (saying), If thou art come
in order to see me, know that I have fully renounced thee.
And I cannot do otherwise, because of my faith in our
Lord Jesus the Christ. And when he had heard these
things, he departed thence in great rage and vexation.
And he sent to call the wives of the senators and some of
the noble women of the city, and he persuaded them and
sent them to her, that they should enter in and speak with
her words of persuasion and advise her to become his wife.

And when these noble women came to speak to her words
of persuasion and reconciliation, so that she might become
wife to her betrothed, the blessed Basilia replied [in] these
words to the noble women, saying to them : There is a
great difference between the ignorant and the wise people,
for the ignorant do not care to receive good things, nor
do they wish to decline the evil things, but wise men
enquire about good things, and progress towards excellent
things, and suddenly they completely renounce [them].
For if this appear to you to be good, that I should f. 47 a
take for my betrothed a certain mortal and transient
man, how much better will it appear to you, that I should
take to myself the Bridegroom who dieth not, and re-
maineth for ever. I rejoice and exult that in my soul
I have decided this, that I should be betrothed alone to
the Bridegroom who dieth not ; to Him who is our Lord
Jesus the Christ ; and I have committed my soul with
my body to Him : and thus I am eager to keep them
spotless to Him. For I see that everything in this world
is transient and perishing, and its joy lasts but a short
time. Why then have we not hope to get possessions over
which death has no power, and which last for ever ? For
with which of mankind remain the blessings of this world
and comfort him ? those which flourish a little while, and
quickly hastily wither. For this reason ye who have wisdom f. 47 b
and understanding see with the good eye of your minds
and consider what hath been spoken to you by me. Be
not ye now walking in the broad path of the good things
of this world, neither have ye any reliance on what is
seen, to which the weakness and inexperience of men
devotes itself. But [be ye] those who forsake human
things and place their hope in God Almighty, He who
sent His only One, our Lord Jesus the Christ, to us, that
He might show us the way of truth in which we should

walk confidently, and that through Him we might know
the true faith and the perfect love which we have, in
whom we are eager for this true faith, and we have great
solicitude on this account that we may keep it spotless
and blameless, by the strength and the help which is
given to us by the Holy Spirit. Let no man therefore
advise us that I should be neglectful of Him whom
I confess, who is our Lord Jesus the Christ, Son of the

f. 48 a living God, He who was born of Mary the holy Virgin
whilst she remained in her uncontaminated virginity.
For our Lord was born from her by His own will, as a
man ; and was worshipped as a king by the shepherds and
by the Magi. He was submissive as a disciple whilst He
was a learned man and a teacher. He was tempted as a
mortal, and He conquered death as an immortal. He was
sold as a slave, and He came in glory as Lord and God.
He was thought to be a prophet, whilst His Spirit spake
by the prophets. And He was anointed as the Messiah,
whilst He anointed kings and priests and prophets. He
suffered and died as a man, and was raised and arose like
God. But lest men should go on in the footsteps of the
Jews, the crucifiers, whilst all His disciples were together
gazing at Him, He was taken up from them to heaven and
sitteth at the right hand of His Father. They are those
who by their martyrdom have sealed the truth of this ; for
after His ascension to His Father, He gave light and
eyesight to the blind, He offered health to the pained and

f. 48 b the sick. They scared away demons from men by their
commandment and by their seals ; they cleansed the lepers;
they raised the dead ; that by means of all these things
which were done by their hands we may know how much
love and care God has for us. And He wishes for us
that we should be heirs of the kingdom of heaven.

And when the blessed Basilia had spoken all these

glorious things to the noble women who were listening
to her, then suddenly by the love of the Christ their
minds waxed fervent in spirit and they did not wish
henceforth to go to their homes; nor were they minded
to return an answer from themselves to Pompeius. But
when Pompeius had taken the evidence of all these
women of senatorial rank he went before the Emperors,
and cast himself on his face before them, saying, Help
us, O ye Emperors victorious and merciful to us your own
people of Rome, be prompt and put away from this city
the new gods which Eugenia has brought from Egypt.
For there are found gods who prohibit men from begetting
children, and if men are hindered from begetting children f. 49 a
how will there be a renewal to Rome? And how will
the army of the Romans be increased and grow? by
means of which conflicts are carried on, and by which
the victorious right hand of your Divinity subdues in
battle the hosts of the foreign enemies which oppose
it. If therefore conjugal intercourse [be lawful] to us, let
thy majesty command "take thy betrothed bride," and
from to-day and henceforth we shall be at peace, and
the Christians may do as they please.

And when Pompeius had said these things and more
in his accusation, the Emperor Gallienus commanded
[him] to take his betrothed Basilia, and that if she did
not wish to be his wife, she should be slain with the sword.
Then a decree went forth from the Emperor concerning
Eugenia, that she should sacrifice to the gods, but that
if she should contumaciously resist, and should not
wish to sacrifice, she should be tormented with bitter
punishments and with severe tortures, as her temerity
deserved, and at the last she also should be condemned
to death with the sword. Again a command went forth
from the Emperor that if any man of the Christians should f. 49 b

introduce another religion and should not wish to sacrifice
to the gods, he should be deprived of dear life by means
of various tortures.   But the blessed Basilia refused every
day to become the wife of Pompeius her betrothed.   For
many days she was tormented by persuasive words of
many people.   On one day she was harassed by women
of senatorial rank and on another day by women who
were neighbours and relatives, who advised her to obey
the command of the Emperor, and to become the wife of
her betrothed.

And why is it necessary for us to say more?   For by
the wisdom and providence and grace of God which
accompanied and assisted her, she overcame all these
persuasions and blandishments.   Because she was of the
imperial family, and she could not be interrogated and
judged publicly, the Emperor commanded that she should
be beheaded with the sword in the interior of her house,
and according to the commandment of the iniquitous
Emperor her head was taken off with the sword.

f. 50 a   But when the blessed Basilia had died in the confession
of our Lord Jesus the Christ, a commandment went forth
again concerning Proteus and Hyacinthus, that they also
should sacrifice to the gods ; but if they should resist the
commandment and should not wish to sacrifice, they also
should die by the sword.   But when the blessed ones did
not consent at all to sacrifice according to the commandment of the tyrant, severe tortures and bitter torments
were applied to their bodies, [and] at last they were
beheaded with the sword.   And when these blessed ones
had died blissfully in the confession of our Lord Jesus the
Christ, the blessed Eugenia also was apprehended and
brought before Anicetus, Eparch of the city.   And he
commanded that she should go immediately and sacrifice
to the goddess Artemis.

But when the blessed Eugenia came to that place and went into the temple she turned to the east and lifted up her hands to heaven and prayed for a long time. Now when she had finished her prayer, the image of Artemis fell and was broken, and it was ground so fine that even its powder could not be perceived. But those who did not f. 50 b understand the power of God, thought it the craft of magic ; and he commanded that they should tie a great stone on the neck of the blessed Eugenia and that she should be thrown into the river Tiber. But when they carried her and threw her in, immediately her bonds were broken, and the stone which they had hung round her neck fell ; but the blessed Eugenia was walking and going on the top of the water. Now when all the Christians saw this great sign that took place, they were filled with joy and exultation, and they praised God with a loud voice, saying, Great is the God of truth, who hath helped Eugenia His handmaiden, and hath not left her to perish, as He was with Peter in the sea, and did not leave him to sink. But when she went and came on the water, and reached the banks of the river, and emerged and stood on the firm land, the servants of the tyrant seized her immediately and conveyed her to prison. But the Eparch commanded that the bath which is called f. 51 a of Severianus should be heated strongly until its colour became like the colour of iron which is heated in the fire ; and that she should be cast in there and perish and be consumed by the blast of the flame. And when the command of the tyrant was fulfilled, they brought the blessed one and threw her into that bath. But immediately when she entered into it, the flame of the fire was quenched before her, so that henceforth it could not be kindled through the great cold that was in it by the commandment of God.

But when the handmaid of the Christ had conquered also this device of the erring ones, he commanded that she should go to the prison; and there be cast into the dark cell, and that no bread and no water should be given to her. But when she entered into the house, that house was immediately filled with great light. And the blessed Eugenia was in that prison twenty days, whilst that light shone there every day. And an angel of the Lord appeared to her, strengthening her and saying, Hail to thee, O

f. 51 b

handmaid of God, Eugenia, for our Lord Jesus the Christ, He whom thou hast loved with all thy heart, and hast served with all thy soul, hath sent me[1] to thee, and saith, Be courageous and be strong, Eugenia, for to-day thou shalt ascend to heaven, gaining the victory over the enemy.

But on that day, which was the birth-day of the Christ, the Eparch commanded that one of the executioners should go, and there in the prison slay her with the sword. And when the blessed one had died[2] by means of the sword in the prison according to the command of the Eparch, the Christians heard (of it) and they came and took up the body of the holy Eugenia, and they carried it in triumph as something they had found, and laid it in a beautiful place which was not far from the city, on the road which is called the Latina.

Now her mother Claudia was sitting at the grave and weeping. And the blessed Eugenia appeared to her and said to her, Rejoice and exult, my mother, for our Lord Jesus the Christ has exalted me to the rest and joy of the saints;

f. 52 a

and has placed my father Philip in the host of just and righteous fathers. And as for thee, on the coming first day of the week[3] He will receive thee in peace. And command my brothers, Avita and Sergius, to keep the seal of the Christ which they have received, that by means of it they may be worthy to become partakers and heirs of the king-dom of heaven, with all the martyrs and confessors. But

---

[1] Cod. "us."   [2] Literally "was crowned."   [3] Or "Sunday."

Claudia went up to her house, and informed her sons according as the blessed Eugenia had informed [her]. And on the first day of the week as they were consummating the glorious mysteries of the divinity, while she was standing in the church and praying, she committed her spirit to the Lord of all spirits, who is our Lord Jesus the Christ; and her sons took her up, and laid her beside their sister, whilst they also excelled in good works and were pleasing to God, so that they converted many of the heathen from the impure sacrifices of idols; and taught them to believe in our Saviour and Redeemer, in[1] our Lord Jesus the Christ. And they received with joyful delight those who went f. 52 b down to the baptismal font of holiness and were cleansed from their crimes and their sins, and gave them rest in their houses. But they did not cease to save every day the souls of men from the captivity of the dragon, the accursed calumniator, and they brought them near to the Christ their Lord. But they also were counted worthy to imitate the excellent deeds of their father, and of their sister; and to inherit the portion and the bliss of the saints together with them. For they pleased the Christ in their life; and they entered and mingled with the glorious hosts of the just and the righteous. May we also be worthy to be heirs with them of the kingdom of heaven, by the grace and tender mercy of our Lord Jesus the Christ! with whom also to the Father be glory and honour and praise and exaltation with the Holy Spirit now and in all time for ever and ever. Amen.

Here endeth the testimony of the blessed Eugenia, and of all the holy martyrs who were martyred with her: Glory to the Hidden One who was made manifest in our body; and we have seen Him who is invisible, visible in our body[2].

---

[1] Literally "on."   [2] Or "in our visible body."

THE story of the excellent life of Pelagia the harlot, who was of the city of Antioch in Syria.

MARY.

f. 70 a AGAIN the story of the Blessed Mary, who was called Marinus.

Glory and praise and adoration to God the Lover of men. He whose door is opened at all times to the repentant; and to him who does not enter the hindrance is in himself. For God doth not reject men, as Peter also, the chief of the Apostles, saith: Of a truth I have perceived that God is no respecter of persons, but in all nations he who feareth Him and worketh righteousness, is accepted of Him. And Ezekiel the prophet: God saith: I desire not the death of the wicked, saith the Lord of lords, but that he should turn from his wicked way and live. And the chosen Apostle Paul makes known concerning our Lord, that He wishes every man to repent, saying in the Epistle to Timothy, I entreat thee, therefore, that before all things f. 70 b thou shouldest offer prayer and supplication and thanksgiving to God on behalf of all men, on behalf of kings and great men that we may lead a peaceable and quiet life in all godliness and purity. For this is good and acceptable before God our Saviour, He who will have all men to be saved, and turn to the knowledge of the truth. For there is one Mediator between God and man, our Lord Jesus the Christ, He who gave Himself a ransom on behalf of all

men. For the door of the house of God is open, as we
have said; and every one who will worketh in the vineyard
of righteousness; not only men but also women, must,
[in spite of] the weakness which attaches to them, enter
into the kingdom. Women have been celebrated in all
generations, and they have even surpassed men. A few
in number will be mentioned by us in this treatise.

Miriam the sister of Moses was called a prophetess.
She led Israel of old, and by her hands God wrought
redemption for Israel. And again by the hand of Judith
He delivered them. And Hanna was called the prophetess
because of the many years that she sat in the temple of the
Lord in holiness until she became worthy to carry the Lord
on her arm. By holiness man comes near to God, as the
Apostle says, Follow after holiness, without which no man   f. 71 a
shall see God. By this many women have prospered.
One of them was the blessed Mary, who is the subject
of the story which we commence. And behold, we begin
to narrate the story of her excellent life and her power of
endurance, this wonderful blessed one, worthy of praise.

There was a certain man in Bithynia, and he had a
wife who bore him one only daughter; and he called her
name Mary. Now after the departure of her mother from
this world, her father reared her with sedulous teaching,
and in honourable life. But when she arrived at full
stature, he said to her, My daughter, behold everything
that I have is given into thy hands. For I am going away
to care about my soul. But when the girl heard this from
her father, she answered and said to him, Father, thou art
seeking to save thy soul; but to destroy my soul. Dost
thou not know that it was said by our Lord, " I lay down
my life for my sheep"? And again, He said that He who
"redeems the soul is as He who created it." But when her
father had heard these things from her, his love was

aroused by her words, the more when he saw her thus weeping and mourning. He spake thus to her, My daughter, what is there that I can do to thee? Thou art a

woman. I am thinking of entering a monastery that I may be removed from the snares of this world, and thou, how canst thou be with us? for the devil will contend with thee more readily, and . . . . . . with the servants of God. But when the girl heard [this], she returned him an answer, and said, No, sir, I shall not enter the monastery thus, as thou hast said, but I will shave the hair from my head and I will clothe myself in the dress of a man, and then I will enter the monastery with thee. Now when he was inclined to be persuaded by the words of his daughter, he distributed and gave everything he possessed to the poor, and he shaved off the hair from the head of his daughter and clothed her, as she had said, in the dress of a man, and changed her name, and called her Marinus[1]. Now when all these things were effectually accomplished, he was continually warning her, [and] saying to her: Look, my daughter, how thou keepest thyself. Like straw in the midst of fire, thus art thou ready to conduct thyself in the midst of the brethren, and the rather that no woman has ever entered the monastery. Keep thyself therefore spotless to the Christ, that we may finish our confession to Him. When he had said these things to her, he led her and entered into the convent. Day by day, as it may be said, this wonderful girl gained the admiration of all, whilst she was perfect in all virtues, that is to say, in obedience, humility, and great devotion, with the others. She spent a little while in the monastery.

The brethren imagined that she was a eunuch because she had no beard, and also because of the softness of her voice; but others thought that she had hurt herself by too great toils in devotion.

---

[1] Cod. "Marina."

Now it happened that her father departed from the world, and she increased the more her deeds, and her obedience and her piety; so that she even received gifts of grace from God, against demons and against various sufferings. And when she placed her hand on the sick, she obtained without delay healing for them by the help of God. Now there were in that convent brethren, holy men, forty in number. And every month four of the brethren were sent on account of the business of the monastery, because there were other monasteries as well as their own, so that they were continually going out visiting and providing [for it]. Now it happened that there was a certain inn about the middle of the road on which they usually travelled, where those who were sent on the business of the convent entered and lodged. And it was not easy to travel over all the road in a single day. But the innkeeper took them in with great solicitude, serving them well, and gave them a place of refuge apart in the garden. Now on a certain day the Abbot called Marinus[1] and said to him: My brother, I am convinced of the sincerity of thy life, and I know that thou art perfect in it all; namely, in humility and in the sedulous- f. 72 b ness of thine obedience. Turn therefore and go forth on the visiting of the monastery, for even the brethren are perplexed that thou art never away on its business. When thou shalt do this, and shalt be obedient, and go out, thou shalt receive a yet greater reward from God. And when the humble one heard these things from the Abbot, he immediately fell at his feet, saying to him: Pray for me, father, and I will go altogether as thou hast commanded me. Now when the event occurred, and Marinus[1] went forth with three brethren, for the visiting of the monastery, they lodged in the above-mentioned inn.

[1] Cod. "Marina."

And while they were there it happened that a certain
soldier seduced the daughter of the innkeeper, so that
she became pregnant by him.   And the soldier who did
this vile deed, said to the daughter of the innkeeper,
being instigated by the devil: If this should become
known to thy father, say to him: "That young monk
slept with me." But day by day she grew larger, so
that her father became aware that a vile thing had happened to his child.   And when he knew it, he demanded
it from her hands, and said: How hath this evil happened
to thee?   Then she threw the blame on Marinus[1], saying:
The monk whom ye praise for being holy did this to
me, and by him I am with child.   Then her father went
to the monastery, and bursting in, he said: Where is

f. 73 a   the deceitful Christian about whom ye say that he is
holy?   But when one of the superintendents received
him, according to their custom, with a greeting, saying to
him: Thou hast done well in coming, brother.   What
is the matter with thee, and why art thou so flurried?
Tell us what has happened to thee, he called out the
more, saying, The hour was an evil one in which I
made your acquaintance.   But when these things were
made known to the Abbot, he inquired and was eager
to calm the tumult in the heart of the innkeeper, and
to learn exactly what the kind of accusation was.   But
he raised his voice all the more, saying, May I never
again see a monk on the earth! and many things like
these, he said.   And when the Abbot had interrogated
him again, to learn from him what was the reason of
the commotion in the business, he said to him, Tell
me, brother, what is the reason of thine accusation? so
that I also may apologize to thee.   Then that innkeeper
answered and said: What thou dost request me I shall tell

[1] Cod. "Marina."

thee. I had one only daughter, with whom I expected my old age to repose, and behold, see what Marinus[1] has done to me, he of whom ye say that he is blessed. He seduced her and behold! she is with child. But when the Abbot had heard these things from him, he was astonished, and said to him, What can I do to thee, my brother, since he is not here, he is away visiting, but nevertheless he is disgraced, so that at his arrival there is nothing for me to do, but to chase him from the monastery.

f. 73 b

Now when Marinus[1] came to the monastery with the three brethren who were with him, the Abbot said to him: Tell me, my brother, are these thy manners? is this thy piety? is this thy humility? Behold, thou hast disgraced my monastery. This innkeeper came and spoke thus against thee. When ye did lodge in his inn, thou didst seduce his daughter, and, lo! her father has made us a spectacle to the world. Tell me, is this the way in which thou didst confess the Christ? is this thy profession? hast thou shown this way of life to thy brethren? is this virtue?

Now when Marinus heard these things, he threw himself on his face on the ground, crying out with bitter weeping, and with choking tears, and he said to the Abbot, Forgive me, father, for the sake of our Lord, because I have transgressed as a human being. But the Abbot, being angry with him, turned him out of the monastery, saying: Enter not our monastery again. Then he went out of the monastery and sat down outside, enduring the cold and the heat. And those who were going in and out of the monastery inquired of him, saying: For what cause dost thou sit outside the door of the monastery? and he answered, Because of my sin, for I have committed fornication, and I am driven away from the monastery. But when the time was fulfilled, and the day arrived that the daughter of the

---

[1] Cod. "Marina."

innkeeper should give birth, she bare a male child.   And the
father of the girl took it up and brought it to the monastery :

and when he found Marinus[1] sitting outside the door of the
monastery, he threw down the baby before him, saying :
Take thy son, whom thou hast wickedly begotten ; and
he left it with him, and went away.   Then Marinus[1] took
up the baby and lamented, saying: O Lord my God ! if I
am requited according to my sins, for what reason should
this poor baby die here with me ?   And Marinus[1], being
disturbed in this way, began to bring milk from the shepherds to the baby, that he might rear the boy as its father.
But it was not enough for Marinus[1] that he had borne this
accusation, but the boy stained his clothes with much weeping.   And the blessed Marinus[1] endured this pain and this
grief for three years.   Now at the end of three years the
brethren took pity on Marinus[1], and said to the Abbot, All
this indignity has been enough for him, for he confesses
his sin before all men.   And, moreover, after sitting there
for three years, he offers repentance to God, as one who
hath been led astray by the devil.   And when the Abbot
was not persuaded to receive him, all the brethren spake,
saying : Unless thou wilt receive him, we also will go
forth from the monastery.   For we cannot look at him any

longer, lying destitute at the door of the monastery, and
not take pity on him.   We suffer from his distress, and
if we did not, how could we implore God about our sins ?
For we see that, behold, during three years he has been
outside the door of the monastery, and he is afflicted and
in great want.   But when the Abbot heard these things
he said to them : Henceforth because of your love I will
receive him.   And the Abbot called Marinus[1] and said unto
him, Thou art not worthy that thou shouldst ever enter
this monastery because thou hast spoiled the rule of the

_____
[1] Cod. " Marina."

monastery by the sin which thou hast committed. But, nevertheless, on account of the love of the brethren, I will receive thee. Thou shalt be the last of them all by the rule of the monastery. But Marinus[1] threw himself on the ground and said : Even that, my lord, will be a great thing for me, that thou hast deemed me worthy to enter within the door of the monastery. Whereas I transgressed and committed fornication, so that, at least thus while I serve the holy fathers, I may become worthy by means of their prayers of a little forgiveness for what I have done amiss. And after these things the Abbot set him to the ignominious tasks of the monastery. And he fulfilled them with great assiduity. But he called to the boy and he followed him and he wept and cried, Father, father ; with the rest of the things that children have to ask for ...... their food. But the alms[2] which Marinus[1] acquired were not sufficient to feed the boy ; he was in great distress because of his nourishment. And when the boy before him attained to f. 75 a full stature, he conducted himself in the monastery with the assiduity of a high order of excellence. · For no man remains in the initial childhood (of mind) in which he is born. But as he is taught he grows up, and this boy became worthy of the monastic garb. But after a little while, on a certain day the Abbot asked the brethren, saying, Where is Marinus[1], for lo ! I have not seen him for three days at the offering ? for he was always found there before every one else at the service. Go, therefore, into his cell, and see if perchance he is in some sickness. And when the brethren entered they found him dead. And they told it to the Abbot, saying : Poor Marinus[1] is asleep. Then he said : How is that? How did his poor soul depart ? What excuse did he make before God ? And when the Abbot had said these things, he commanded that they

---

[1] Cod. " Marina."   [2] Literally " consolations."

should dress him. But when the brethren went to dress
him, according to the commandment of the Abbot, they
found that he was a woman. And when they saw her,
their limbs became weak, and the light of their eyes was
troubled. And immediately when they had rested a little,
they began crying, Kyrie eleison. But the Abbot, when
he heard the voice of the cry, inquired in order that he
might learn what was the reason of their cry. And they
said to him, Brother Marinus[1] is a woman. And when he

f. 75 b
came and saw her, he was seized with great amazement also,
at what endurance she had possessed; and he fell on his
face on the ground, and cried with choking tears, saying,
Forgive me: I have sinned against God and against thee.
I will die here before thy holy feet, until I receive forgiveness for my sins which I committed against thee. And he
said other things like these, and more than these, lying
on his face at the feet of the saint, with sobs and with
weeping for three days. But at the end of three days,
a voice came to him, saying: If thou hadst done
these things intentionally to me this sin would not have
been forgiven thee. But, nevertheless, the sin is forgiven
thee, because thou didst commit it unwittingly. Then
when the Abbot rose from before the feet of the saint,
he sent for the innkeeper and they brought him. And
when he came the Abbot said to him: Behold, poor
Marinus[1] is dead. But when the innkeeper heard it, he
answered and said: God forgive him! for he disgraced
my house. Then the Abbot said to him: May God
forgive thee, because thou hast troubled me also and
my monastery. Do not remain henceforward in sin, but
repent. For thou hast sinned before God, and hast also
made me to sin. Thou didst incite me with thy words,
and I sinned by thy fault. For although Marina's know-

---

[1] Cod. "Marina."

ledge and her dress were those of a man, by nature she f. 76 a
was a woman. But when the innkeeper heard that she
was a woman, he was amazed and was seized with astonishment at these things which were said, and he still remained
incredulous. Then the Abbot led him by the hand and
showed him his unbelief, what he had said to him. Then
the innkeeper also began with many tears to confess his
sin, which he had committed unwittingly. And whilst this
commotion was going on they dressed her sacred body, and
laid her in an honourable place with a beautiful service, and
with much glory inside of the monastery, and they praised
God who had endowed her with such endurance. But at
the conclusion of all these things came the daughter of the
innkeeper, worried by a demon; and she confessed all the
truth, saying, It was a soldier who committed this im-
purity with me and made me pregnant, and advised me to
wrong the handmaid of God, and the monastery. And
whilst that girl said these things she was cured without
delay by the grave of the holy Mary. And they all
praised our Lord for the occurrence and for the sign
that had happened, He who hath given such endurance to
those who love Him, that she persevered thus until death
and never revealed herself to any one as a woman. May
we also, my beloved ones, emulate in perseverance and in
endurance the manly woman so that our Lord may give f. 76 b
us grace and mercy with her and the portion of the
saints in the fearful day of judgment, by our Lord Jesus
the Christ, to whom with His Father and His living and
Holy Spirit be glory and honour and adoration for ever
and ever.

Here endeth the story of the blessed Mary: Marinus.

EUPHROSYNE.

AGAIN, the story of Euphrosyne of Alexandria.

Now there was once upon a time in the great city of Alexandria a certain honourable man whose name was Paphnutius, and he was assiduous in fulfilling the command-ments of God. And he took a wife who was modest and worthy of his choice, and she was of a well-known and honourable family, and she was barren and she did not bear [a child]; and her husband was in much concern and in sore vexation, because he had no son to whom he might leave his wealth, after his departure from the world, to dispose of his wealth properly to the needy. But when his wife saw her husband was vexed, she rested neither by night nor by day, being continually in the churches imploring with fasting and with prayer that God would grant her a child. She gave great wealth to the poor and to the sick, and distributed it to holy dwellings and to monasteries. And in that city her husband also, when he passed by the churches and the monasteries, groaned and desired that he might meet with a monastery and might find a man who was worthy before God who was likely by means of his prayer to persuade God to grant him the desire of his heart. And at last he went to a certain monastery in which there was a famous Abbot. A certain great God-fearing monk was in it. And when he entered that monastery he gave him a benediction and he sat in an expansive and protracted conversation with the Abbot and with the brethren who were sitting with him. Then after a little while he revealed his secret to the Abbot, and he was

inclined to his request that they should persuade God
on his behalf, to grant them fruit of their loins. And
God took pity on the request of the two and granted
them one daughter.

Now when Paphnutius saw the good government and
modest life of the Abbot, he did not go away from that
convent. On this account also he brought his wife many
times there to be blessed by the Abbot and by the brethren
who were with him. When the girl was weaned and was
about six years old they baptized her and called her name
Euphrosyne. But her parents rejoiced greatly that she was
beloved by God and was beautiful of countenance and was
very lovely in her aspect.

Now when she was thirteen years old her mother departed from the world, and her father continued to educate
and teach her in the Scriptures and the wisdom of God. f. 77 b
But the girl was worthy to be on the right side by nature
and as the fruit of prayer. And she loved instruction to
such a degree that her father admired her because of it.
And her name was spread abroad in all the city because
of her wisdom and love of learning. But yet more because
of the great development of her stature, and the splendid
beauty of her countenance. And many great and powerful
men were attracted to love her, to betroth her as a bride
for their sons, and many came to her father in order
to get an advantage over each other in betrothing her
to their sons. But he said to them, Let the will of
God be done. Now one of the great men who was
more excellent than them all in power, and in might,
called her father and spoke with him about the matter;
and [her father] was persuaded and betrothed her to his
son, and he gave her a betrothal present. But a short
time afterwards, when she was about eighteen years of age,
her father led her and conducted her to that monastery,

and carried with her all good things to do honour to the
Abbot and to the brethren who were with him. And
whilst he was talking with them he said to the Abbot:
Behold, I have brought to you the fruit of your prayers
about which you prayed. If God wills, I wish to give her
to a husband. And the Abbot commanded that they
should lodge him in the hospice for strangers of the
convent, whilst he talked with the girl and blessed her
and prayed for her. And he talked of many things with
her about purity and virginity and the fear of God. And
she progressed very greatly in her learning. When she
had been in the convent three days she listened to the
singing of their daily service, and she saw the beautiful
assiduity of their conduct and she wondered at their
virtues, saying, Blessed are these elect ones because that
although they are in the world they have the likeness of
angels; and after their departure from this world they
are worthy of eternal life. And she began to repent in
her heart, because of the fear of God.

f. 78 a

But after three days Paphnutius said to the Abbot:
Command, O spiritual father, concerning thy handmaiden
that she may come to thee, and grant her the prayer of
thy mouth. For it is our desire to go to the city. But
when she came into the Abbot's presence, Euphrosyne
threw herself down before his feet, saying to him, I
beseech thee, father, pray for me that God may redeem
my soul. And the Abbot raised his hands and said:
God who knowest everything when it has not yet been,
do Thou lead this Thy handmaid to grace, that she may
please Thee and may be worthy to find a portion and an
inheritance with those who please Thee. And they took
leave of the Abbot and went away to their city. But
her father, when he saw a hermit in the city, received
him and brought him into his house, and persuaded him

f. 78 b

to pray for him and his daughter. But a certain day came when there was to be the commemoration of the monastery. And the Abbot sent a certain brother to bring Paphnutius to the commemoration and the vigil of the monastery. And when this brother went to his house and asked about him the young men said that he had gone out. But when Euphrosyne learnt about the arrival of that recluse she called him and recognized him, saying to him, "About how many brethren are there in that monastery?" And he said to her, "Three hundred and fifty-two." And she said to him, "Whosoever therefore wishes to go and dwell there, do they receive him, O father? And do you all therefore sing in one church? And do you keep one fast?" The recluse said to her, "The music is sung by all of us in a congregation, but each [keeps] the fast as he wishes and can endure."

Then when she had inquired about all the affairs of the monastery she said to the recluse, "I could have wished that I were able to go out from this vain world, but I fear that my father wishes to give me to husbands because of the vain wealth of this world." The recluse said to her, "Nay, my daughter, let not a man dishonour thy body, and do not surrender such beauty to shameful passion, but be thou altogether in thy purity a bride to the Christ, who is able to give thee instead of these transitory f. 79 a. things the kingdom of heaven. Therefore shave thy head in secret and go to the monastery and thou shalt be saved." Now when she had heard these words she said to the hermit, "And who will shave me? for I do not wish to be shaved by laymen, for they do not keep secrets." The hermit said to her, "Behold I am about to take thy father to the monastery, and he will be there three or four days. Thou therefore send and call one of the recluses and thus as thou desirest he will arrange for thy comfort." But

whilst Euphrosyne and the hermit were talking her father
also arrived. And when Paphnutius saw the hermit, he
recognized him and asked him, "What is the reason of the
work of God's love in thee towards us?" The recluse
said to him, "It is the vigil and commemoration of the
monastery, and our father the Abbot sent us that thou
shouldest come and enjoy his prayers with us." And when
Paphnutius, the father of Euphrosyne, had heard it he
rejoiced greatly. And he carried with him what was
necessary for many days, and put it into a ship whilst he
went to the monastery. And when Paphnutius arrived at
that monastery he was blessed by the Abbot. And while
Paphnutius was in the monastery Euphrosyne sent one of
her faithful servants to the church where the recluses were
assembled, the one which was called of Theodosius, and
said to that young man, "Look for the first hermit who
meets thee in the church, take him and bring him to this
place." And when the young man had gone as he was
bidden, as if it were by the doing of God a very old
man met him who was from Scete. Now when the boy
who was sent by Euphrosyne saw the old man, he took
him and brought him to her. And when the girl saw him
she said to him, "Pray for me, father." And when he had
prayed for her he sat down. But she said to the old man,
"Father, I have a father and he is a servant of God, and
he has great riches, and he had a wife and from her he
begat me; and he wishes because of his riches to marry
me in this sinful world. And I do not at all wish to be
contaminated by the pollution of this world, and on the
other hand I fear to rebel against my own father: and what
I shall do I know not. For all this night I have been
awake on account of this; whilst I implored of God that
He would make known to me what is profitable for my
poor soul. And after the light had dawned it was shown to

f. 79 b

me that I should send to the church, and should fetch the
first hermit who met me. And behold, as if by the
guidance of God, thou hast been sent to us, and now I
would persuade thee, father, teach me what will help me."

But when the old man had heard these words from her
he began to talk with her, saying, "And what dost thou
wish my daughter? When our Lord saith that whosoever f. 80 a
hateth not his father and his mother and his brethren
and his sisters, and even his own life, he cannot be my
disciple. But what business have I to say more than this
to thee? If therefore thou art able to endure the temptations of the adversaries, leave everything and flee; for to
the wealth of thy parents many heirs will be found. Lo!
there are churches, and there are asylums for the poor, and
there are prisons, and there are hospices, and there are
monasteries, and there are orphans, and there are widows,
and there are lepers, and there are sick people, and there
are prisoners; let thy father leave them to whatsoever
place it may please him. But only do not thou lose thy
soul."

Euphrosyne said to him: "I hope in God by your
prayers, that I am eager to save my soul." The old
man said to her, "My daughter, if thou wilt do this,
do it quickly, without delay, lest thou be prevented and
prohibited through negligence from this beautiful purpose of thy heart." The girl said to the old man, "I
brought thee here, my lord, for this purpose, that thou
mightest accomplish the desire of my soul." And forthwith the old man rose up, engaged in prayer, shaved
her, dressed her in a robe and prayed for her, saying,
"May God who hath redeemed all the saints keep thee
from evil." And when the old man had said these things
he departed from her. Then Euphrosyne considered and
said, "If it be that I am to go to a convent of women

f. 80 b   my father will never cease to seek till he has found me, and
he will snatch me away by force from the convent on
account of my betrothed. But I will put myself into a
domicile of men, in a place where no one will suspect
me." And she took off women's clothes and wrapped
herself in the garb of a man. And when it was evening
she went forth from her house, taking with her five hundred
dinars.

And in the morning her father arrived and came to his
city, and as if it were by the direction of God he went at
once to the church. And Euphrosyne his daughter went
to the very monastery which her father loved. And
she talked with the porter and said to him, "Brother, if it
please thee, go and say to the Abbot that a certain
eunuch from the palace is at the door outside and desires
to speak to thee." And when the porter had entered and
related her business to the Abbot, he commanded him to
enter. And when he had entered, he threw himself down
and did penance. And after a prayer had been offered
they sat down. The Abbot said to her: "Why has the
love of God that is in thee made thee trouble thyself about
us?" She replied to him, "Father, I am from the palace,
and I had a love for the garb of a recluse: and I knew our
city does not know very well that a monastic community
dwells in it. And I heard about thy Holiness and about
this monastery, and I am come to be with you if it please
you to accept me. I have great wealth, and if we are seated
on our seats in the quiet of this dwelling I will bring it to
f. 81 a   the door." The Abbot said to him: "Thou hast done well
in coming, my son: behold the monastery is before thee, if
it seem good in thine eyes, abide with us." And again the
Abbot said to him: "My son, what is thy name?"
"Esmeraldus," he replied. The Abbot said, "Since thou
art so young, and thou canst not dwell alone, it is expedient

for thee to have an older man with thee, that he may teach thee the rule of monasticism." "I will do as thou desirest," said the blessed one. And Esmeraldus brought out the five hundred dinars and gave them into the hands of the Abbot, saying, "Take these, father, and do as thou wilt with them, and if I know that I can live quietly here, I will bring also the remainder."

Then the Abbot called a certain brother whose name was Agapius, a sensible man, and delivered over Esmeraldus to him, saying, "Let this man be henceforth thy son and thy disciple." And he bent the knee and prayed, and Agapius took him away to his cell because his face was covered with beauty like an emerald. And when he came into the refectory Satan made many to stumble at his beauty, so that they complained against the Abbot, that he had received such a fair and beautiful face into the monastery, and when the Abbot learnt it he called for Esmeraldus and said to him, "The fair beauty of thy face has occasioned many falls to those who are not well-established. I therefore desire thee to dwell in a separate cell at some distance from [the monastery] and thou mayest f. 81 b be quiet and sing hymns there and eat; and do not let thyself be seen by the brethren." And he ordered Agapius to prepare a separate cell so that Esmeraldus might dwell in it.

Then Agapius did all that he was commanded to do by the Abbot, and he conducted Esmeraldus and led him into a cell. And whilst he was occupying this cell he was very zealous and constant in fasting, vigil, and prayer, and in sleeping on the ground, and in the reading of the sacred Scriptures; and was praising God by night and by day, so that Agapius saw the assiduity of Esmeraldus and the great excess of his humility, and was amazed. He related to the brethren all about his great zeal, and by this they made progress and were instructed.

But the father of Euphrosyne arrived at dinner-time and went into his house. And when he did not find his daughter he asked his servants, "Where is Euphrosyne, my daughter?" And they said to him, "We saw her last evening, but since the morning we have not seen her." Then her father thought that perhaps her betrothed had come and taken her away; and he sent to inquire about this matter. But when the father of her betrothed and his son heard this they were greatly disquieted, and they arose and came in haste to the house of Paphnutius, and found that he had flung himself on the earth and was in tears. And he said, "Perhaps some man has deceived her and taken her away and fled with her." He sent horsemen instantly through all Egypt and to the provinces, and he sent ships and skiffs on the sea in quest of her, and the nunneries and the churches and the caves and the deserts were searched; and they inquired about her of their friends and neighbours, and they searched for her over all the city. But no searcher found her.

f. 82 a

Now when they had sought for her in every place and had not found her, they wailed and wept for her as for one dead. The father-in-law wept for his daughter-in-law, the father wailed for his daughter, saying, "Woe is me, my fondly loved daughter! Woe is me for the light of my eyes! Woe is me for the consolation and solace of my soul! Who is he that hath robbed me of my treasure? Who is he that hath snatched away my nestling? Who is he that hath scattered my wealth? Who is he that hath carried away the beauty and ornament of my house? Who is he that hath entered and robbed me of my own hope? Which wolf has snatched away my sheep? What place hides the beauty that is like the sun? What abyss holds captive from me that royal seal? For she was to be the raiser up of my race. She was the staff of my old age.

She was my rest in labours. She was the repose of my troubles. She it was who lightened my miseries. O earth! cover not the blood of my darling till I learn who has turned my joy into sorrow."

Now when Paphnutius' friends and neighbours heard how he wept for his daughter, and wailed for her in such words, they also wailed and wept for her with a loud voice, until the whole city was stirred by the noise of their mourning and wept for the sudden loss of the young girl.

Now when Paphnutius had come to acquiesce in the inexorable nature of his sorrow, he went to the monastery, f. 82 b and threw himself at the feet of the Abbot, saying to him, "I beg of thee, my father, do not neglect prayer to God until they find the effects of thy prayers. Thy hand-maiden, my daughter, has been abducted." And when the Abbot heard this he was greatly troubled, and he commanded them to beat the wooden gongs, so that the brethren might be assembled. And when they had come together, he said to them, "Brethren, make [a confession of] sins, and appoint a sabbath, and fast every two days, and strive with God, and beg Him to reveal and disclose to us where is the daughter of Paphnutius." But when they had fasted all the sabbath, God did not reveal the matter to any one of them, because her own prayers overcame the prayers and vigils of all the brethren. For she had striven with God, and had persuaded Him not to dis-close anything concerning her in her lifetime. For all the brethren were sorrowing because God had not revealed this matter to them. But the Abbot encouraged Paphnutius, saying, "Do not afflict thyself, nor grieve, but thank God, and whatever He wills He will make known to thee con-cerning her, for thou knowest that she has not devoted herself to any evil, but to good; and for this reason God does not wish to make known what concerns her to any of us. If she had been about any evil, God would not have been neglectful of thy labours, and of those of the holy men who are amongst us." And when Paphnutius heard this he was a little quieter in his affliction and went away to his

f. 83 a   city praying that God would make him worthy of the good and beautiful home[1]. Then after a little while he again went to that monastery and paid his respects to the brethren and returned to his city. On one of the days when he went to the monastery the Abbot said to him, "I want you to talk with a certain good brother from the palace of the Emperor Theodosius." Paphnutius replied, "Father, I am content," and the Abbot sent and called Agapius his chief [monk] and said to him, "Take my lord Paphnutius and lead him to brother Esmeraldus, so that he may profit by him. And he took him and conducted him thither." But when Euphrosyne saw her father she was all bathed in her tears. But her father imagined that penitence was the reason of her tears. He did not recognize her in the very least, for her beauty was withered up by her much fasting, and her vigils, and by her sleeping on the ground, for she had covered up her face in a rug, so that her father might not recognize her by some tokens. When they had engaged in prayer he sat down and she began to talk to him about mercy and righteousness and love and chastity, and about the freedom of souls, and while Esmeraldus was speaking the heart of Paphnutius was moved, and he was full of tears. And he was impelled by his love to embrace her. But he was ashamed

f. 83 b   of it, and restrained himself. So while they were speaking to each other about things profitable to the soul, Paphnutius went away from Esmeraldus, and going to the Abbot, said to him, "Glory be to God, O father, for how much have

---

[1] Or "conduct."

I profited by this man. God [only] knows how my soul has been captivated by his love, as if he had been Euphrosyne my daughter." And he took leave of the brethren and returned to his city.

Now when Esmeraldus had been in the monastery for thirty-eight years, he fell ill of the sore sickness which was the cause of [his] death. And during his sickness Paphnutius also arrived and came to that monastery. And after he had talked as usual with the Abbot, he said to him, "My lord, I wish to see Esmeraldus, whom my soul loves fondly." And the Abbot sent and called for Agapius and said to him, "Take my lord Paphnutius and conduct him to our brother Esmeraldus, for it seems to me that he will not again see him in life." And when Paphnutius went he fell on the rug on which Esmeraldus was lying and kissed his feet, saying, "Pray for me, brother, that God may give me consolation concerning my daughter, for my soul is not yet healed of its grief (about her)." Esmeraldus said to him, "Do not grieve, and do not weep, for whilst thou art here God will disclose and make known to thee [something] concerning thy daughter. But I advise thee to stay here for f. 84 a three days, and not to go far away from me." He said to him, "Thou hast commanded and I will certainly do it. I will not go away, I will not leave thee for these three days."

Now when the third day arrived, and he knew therefore that he was departing to his Lord, she said to Paphnutius, "My father, since God has guided me according to His will, and has fulfilled the desire of my soul, I wish that from to-day thou mayest be quit of grief in the matter of Euphrosyne thy daughter. For I am that poor and miserable one, and behold! thou hast seen me, and thou art at rest, and thy wish is fulfilled. But for the sake of our Lord let no one know this. Moreover, do not allow any one else to shroud my body, but thou only, do thou

shroud me. And because I confessed to the Abbot, my
father, when I came here and took upon myself this gentle
yoke, that I possess great wealth, and that being permitted
to sojourn here, I should leave it to those in this monastery, leave it to them, father. And thou also, my father
Paphnutius, knowest this place where we live in the fear
of God, and I beg of thee, my father, pray for me, a
miserable creature."

And when the blessed, holy Euphrosyne had said this
she yielded up her spirit to God. Now when her father
Paphnutius had heard it, he wondered and fainted, and fell
to the ground, and was as one dead. And Agapius, the
master of Esmeraldus, entered and saw that he was already
dead, and he sprinkled water on his face, saying to him,
"What is the matter with thee, my lord Paphnutius?" But
he said to him, "Leave me to die here, for I have seen
glorious things to-day." And when Agapius had raised him
up, he threw himself again on his face, and kissed her, and
drenched her with his tears, crying out and saying, "Woe
is me, my beloved daughter! Woe is me for the light of
my eyes! Wherefore didst thou not disclose this to me
aforetime, that I also might die willingly with thee?
What a great wonder that thou hast despised in such a
way the wickedness of the enemy! how thou hast escaped
from the power of the princes of the darkness of this world,
my daughter, and hast entered into everlasting life!"

Now when Agapius heard these things, a great astonishment fell upon him; and he ran weeping to the Abbot,
and related all the occurrence to him. Now when the
Abbot had heard these things he came in haste and fell upon
the corpse of the holy Euphrosyne weeping, and crying
out and saying : " Bride of the Christ! and holy daughter,
do not disappoint the members of thy community, nor this
holy monastery, but pray and beg from God that He may

f. 84 b

give us understanding that we may direct it courageously and reach the haven of salvation, and enjoy with thee the good things of eternity." And he commanded them to beat the wooden gongs, and to assemble all the communities, and accompany her with great honour. Then when all the communities were congregated to learn about the story of the saint, a great amazement fell upon them all, and they sang praises to God who had done signs and wonders. Then f. 85 a one of the brethren who had only one eye, the other one being closed, stepped in to embrace the body of the saint. And when he put his face to her face, his eye, which was closed, was opened and he saw with it. And when all the brethren saw it they sang praises to God, who is to be admired in His saints and who doeth signs and wonders by their hands, and who hath given the seal of remission and of redemption to those who are willing to take refuge in the love of our Lord Jesus the Christ. And they carried the body of the saint in procession with psalms and hymns as it was fitting. And they put her on the bier of the fathers in a place of honour. Then her father Paphnutius gave all his wealth and his possessions to the churches and to the monasteries, to the poor, the orphans, and the widows. But he gave the greater part of his riches to the monastery in which his daughter Euphrosyne lay. And, moreover, he shut himself up in his daughter's cell. And he had great consolation in the rug upon which his daughter had lain on the ground during her life. And her father lived for ten years in that monastery and departed to his Lord. And he left the things of earth, and was buried by the side[1] of Saint Euphrosyne his daughter; to the glory of the Father, and of the Son, and of the Holy Ghost, to whom be dignity, praise and honour for ever and ever. Amen.

Here endeth the story of Esmeraldus of Alexandria.

---

[1] Literally "over the body."

ONESIMA.

Again, the story of the blessed Onesima[1].

There was a certain blessed woman in Egypt whose name was Onesima, and she was the daughter of the king. And fifteen cities in the world belonged to her parents. And she being their daughter, they placed the crown on her in their lifetime, for they said, "Lest our royal dynasty be obliterated, let him who comes and takes her, establish the kingdom after us." For all the floor of their palace was inlaid with slabs of white marble; and all the walls were embossed with sheep and oxen on planks of cedar-wood and on slabs of ivory, and with plates of bronze, incrusted and embossed with narcissi and lilies. And the girl was brought up in such a manner that she was accustomed to read the Scriptures every day of her life from the third hour till the ninth hour. She was adorned with great beauty, passing that of all other women.

Now one day, whilst she was sitting, reading in the Scripture, [something] came into her mind. And she sighed, and wept, and said: "If God has willed, both my parents may die together, and they have not given me to a husband, and I may fall amidst the troubles of this world." And then a few days afterwards, as if it were by the will of God, both her parents failed and died together. Then the blessed Onesima celebrated

---

[1] MS. Onesimus.

their obsequies in white garments. And after her parents f. 86 a
were at rest and she had come away from the grave,
she went to the church with the crown resting on her
head, and prayed ; then went joyfully home. But many
people were jesting and saying, " It is not proper for a
woman, a virgin, the daughter of a king, to display her
beauty." But the blessed one did not take it to heart.

Now many days afterwards as she was sitting and
reading from the Gospel, she found where our Lord said
to the young man, " Go, sell all that thou hast, and give to
the poor, and take up thy cross, and follow Me ; and thou
shalt have treasure in heaven." Then the blessed Onesima
sighed and wept, and said, " Alas ! that I should have
meditated on divine Scriptures from my childhood and
I have not done the one thing that is beautiful in the sight
of God and of man." And she sent instantly and fetched
lawyers, and bequeathed everything that belonged to her
to the orphans, and to the widows, and to the churches,
and to the hospices ; and she freed her slaves and bond-
maidens ; and she went out and stood at the door of her
palace. And she took her tunic and her veil from off her
head and the girdle of gold from her waist, and the royal
crown, and she flung them down inside the door of her
palace, saying, "Goodbye to you, O wealth of this world ! and
gold, and sin[1], and let the Christ alone be my companion."
Then nothing of the treasures of her ancestors belonged to
the blessed one except the Gospel which lay next to her
bosom. And when she had arrived at a hostelry, she took a f. 86 b
worn-out ragged cloth and put it over her nakedness. Then
the blessed one said in her heart, " It is not fitting that
I should dwell in a place where there are people who
know me, and that they should see me and say, ' It is she
who freed her slaves and her bond-maidens,' and that they

---

[1] MS. gold of sin.

should praise me and that I should exchange the love of the Christ for the glory of this world. I will go away to foreign parts, to where even if I say that something belongs to me, nobody will believe me, and I shall feign myself mad: and no honour will come to me from men, and all who see me will mock me, and despise me, and drive me away. Shall I speak of cultivated land, and not of the desert? But I have read in the Scripture and have glorified God."

Then the blessed one went out to the wilderness and walked for forty parasangs[1]. And [instead of] the great luxury that she had possessed, immediately when the sun touched her it burnt her, like a flower stricken by the summer-heat. And she walked in the wilderness and her blood flowed, and trickled from her footprints while she walked on the stumps of the wilderness. Then the blessed one sat down and read from the Scripture in the wilderness, and the wild beasts came together from every place, and creeping things and flying things and fowls, and they sat at the feet of the blessed one, and listened to the sound of the reading of the Scriptures which lasted from the third hour till the ninth hour; and when she took up the book to carry it with her the beasts would go away from her for nine hours and repair to their pastures. And immediately when they were removed from her to a distance of nine steps, they would find their pasture of every kind suitable to each of them, so that some provender was given to every one, because they were constantly coming to her for many days; and for forty years the beasts kept the fasts with her in the wilderness, sitting beside her constantly, and never going completely away from her. And the food of the blessed one was the fruit of date palms, and she drank water from the fountain, until the appearance of her face was like the colour of sackcloth.

f. 87 a

---

[1] A parasang is a day's journey.

And after she had been for forty years in the desert she said to herself, " Woe is me ! how I am dwelling in comfort, and I am regaled with eating the fruit of the date palms, and I drink water from the fountain, and I resemble the wild ass that treads on the grass, and there is no voice to tame him, and it is not possible to guide him. I, likewise, have no one to quarrel with me, nor to revile me, nor is there a man to laugh with me, nor with whom I can be angry, that I may be requited for it. For if I be without a man who is the guardian of my soul ; I have no recompence, but I will live in the cultivated land in a convent, f. 87 b and I will care for my own soul and for my companions ; and I will wash the feet of the sisters, and will give rest to the weary and to the troubled ; and I will be despised by the sisters, and I will wash the feet of strangers. And I will be scourged by the Abbess, and will endure it from those who are younger than myself. And I will bear reviling because of my love to the Christ. And I shall have a recompence from God. And I will fast. And when I have fasted they will say, ' She has been eating.' And I will abstain from wine, and they will say that I have been drinking at a feast. And I will serve, and they will consider me idle. And I will keep a vigil, and they will call me a sleeper. For if these afflictions do not pass over me, and if I do not endure suffering, and contempt does not pass over me, I shall have no remuneration in the presence of God."

And the blessed Onesima went to the door of a convent, which was called the Convent of the Sedrarum[1], in which there were sisters living three hundred in number ; and she knocked at the door of this convent. And a certain old sister came out and answered her, who had stood at the door for forty years, till her person had become rigid down

---

[1] Or " Anthems."

to her knees from the heaviness of her life and the antiquity of her years.

The aged one answered and said to her, "Why dost thou knock at this door? Tell me, my daughter, what thou wantest, that I may give it to thee. Perhaps thou art in some pain. Can I do anything that would be of use to thee"? And Onesima was silent for seven days and did not give her an answer. And the aged one said, "Alas for this our daughter, she is surely mad! And I know from her appearance, how beautiful she was; although she is spoiled by demons. I will show favour to her for the sake of God; and I will bring her in and shut her up in one of the cells near the door, and no demon shall come from any of the mountains to oppress her." And she brought her in and made her sit down in one of the houses, and put three chains upon her, and said to her, "In the name of the Only Son who was hung upon the Cross, I have put three chains upon thee. May the power of the only Son of God help thee!" And the aged one left her chained near the door, and went in and said to the Abbess, "My Lady! My Lady! this daughter of ours is led captive by Satan, the destroyer of men. And she passed by the door and it has come out by the force of thy prayer and thou hast delivered her from its hands." She commanded her to enter. The Abbess said to her, "What dost thou wish?" "That I may bring in God's afflicted one and wash her feet, that ye may give rest to the weary and the troubled, and to those who carry heavy burdens; and if ye are washing the feet of strangers, may their dust be upon us [as] the filth of our sins."

And the sisters went out with the door-keeper and brought in the blessed one. And she feigned herself mad and did not wish to enter with them. And when they had surrounded her they brought her in by force, and they were going to take the book from her, and they could not

f. 88 a

f. 88 b

get it out of her hands as she did not give it to them. But she feigned herself mad, as one who did not know what they were saying to her. But they were saying to each other, " What is that book which she is carrying, and which she did not allow to be snatched from her hands?" And they tried to wash her feet, and she did not allow them [to do it,] and—like one who was really mad—she tore the clothes of the sisters. And they put questions to her, and she did not answer them. And when they saw her thus, they said to the Abbess, " If she cries out, leave her there, and be cautious about her, lest the evil one come, and throw her into the fire. And they left her in the prison." And she slept there and got up. And there she went in and out and swept the prison-house. And she did work on behalf of every one. And day by day like a person who is kneading dough she was beating with her feet, and crying out as if the demon had come upon her. And she was scourged by the sisters, and was rejoicing in her mind. And day by day she carried a jar of water, and f. 89 a went out to give drink to strangers at the partings of the highways. And day after day she broke the jar in the courtyard of the convent like a person possessed with a demon. And three times a year a place which the sisters went out to of necessity, was thoroughly washed out by her hands, through the sagacity of her mind (and) for the sake of God. And those who came in and who went out beat her and derided her. And she was buffeted by all of them.

And after the lapse of forty years that she had been in the wilderness, and forty years in the prison of the convent, eighty years in all, the angel of God appeared to the blessed Abbot of the Anchorites, who had been shut up in a cell for many years, and said to him, " Dudina, thy service has been pleasing to the guardian angels, and the angels rejoice in thy vigil. Now go out of thy cell, and

go to receive a blessing from a woman who is shut up
in the prison in the convent of the Sedrarum, and thy
service will be doubled again the more with the divine
talent and the merchandise of the Christ." And the blessed
one went forth from his retreat and persuaded the Bishop
and the superintendent to give him leave to go to the
convent, because men did not enter it. And because he
was the Abbot of Abila, and was very excellent in his
life, the Bishop and superintendent did not refuse, nor
forbid him to enter that convent. And when the blessed
one went and arrived at it, the angel of God said to him,
" When thou dost enter the convent, behold all the sisters
have put on hoods ; and the sister about whom thou hast
been told, has a crown of old rags on her head, and she is
all but naked ; approach and receive her blessing." And
the brethren went before him and said to them, " Behold,
the blessed Abbot of the Anchorites has come to receive a
blessing from you." And all the sisters were greatly agitated
with weeping, and said, " Woe to us, for our sins have been
exposed in the presence of God, and the servant of God
is come to curse us. And we shall be condemned by the
just judgment of God."

And when he was about to enter, the sisters went out
to meet him, with psalms and hymns also. But that
sister did not go out with them, because she said in her
heart, " I will feign myself mad, and I will stay quietly in
the prison, and I shall not go out. And he will see me,
and prayer will be made to God for me, (to know) who
I am and whose daughter I am. And he will make it
known to the sisters and he will honour me, and I shall
destroy the work that I have wrought before God."

And all the sisters advanced and saluted him, and were
blessed by him. And when he stood up, he looked here
and there, and that sister did not appear to him amongst

f. 89 b

them, about whom the angel of the Lord had spoken to him. f. 90 a
And he answered and said to the Abbess, "There is one of
your sisters wanting, she is not amongst you, and I desire
to see her." The Abbess replied and said to him, "There
is no sister here, my lord, except one who is mad, and it
is not possible for her to go out, because she is deranged."
And the blessed one said, "Send and fetch her." And
the sisters went in to seek her : but she did not want to go
out with them. And whilst they were dragging her along
and striking her on the face, and sprinkling ashes on her
eyes, and beating her with the besoms of the prison-house
and saying to her, "Get out, wicked demon! behold! thy
demon knows the agent of the Christ who is standing
outside, and it forbids thee to come out lest he should
cast it out from thee." And as they were dragging
her and bringing her out, the blessed saint the Abbot of
the Anchorites saw her, and he ran to meet her, and he
fell down and did obeisance to her, and took off the cowl
from his head and said, "Bless me, my lady!" And the
sisters answered and said to him, "Rise, my lord! she is
a mad woman." And he said to them, "It is ye who
are mad women, but she is the salt which flavours the
savourless, which Satan had made insipid by reason of
sins." And when he had said this to them, they were
pained in their heart, and they repented and opened their
eyes with weeping, and they stripped off the three hundred
veils from their heads. And they threw themselves down
before him and said to him, "My lord, intercede with her,
that she may tread with a holy step on the veils, for there
is not one of us who has not sinned against her." For f. 90 b
there was one saying, "I have certainly beaten her;" and
one said, "I have certainly struck her;" and another said,
"When I washed a dish or a kettle I threw it at her head,
on a day of snow and ice." And saying these things they

came and fell at the feet of the saint and beat their heads
on the ground, saying to her, "Have mercy upon us,
handmaid of God, thou who art entering into the marriage-
supper of light, and persuade the lord of the feast not to
drive us out at the door into outer darkness." And as they
said these things they wept and fell down before her until
the convent became like a field that had been irrigated with
water from the tears of their eyes.

Now the blessed one was inwardly perplexed; but
outwardly she laughed, whilst they were saying these
things to her, till a voice from heaven was heard, saying
to them: "I have accepted, and I accept the tears of
your repentance." And the blessed one heard that voice
speaking to them. And immediately the blessed [man]
led her and took her over these veils to a broad path
in the form of a cross. And he said to them: "May
God give health to your hidden companions!" And he
preached to them from the third hour till the ninth hour;
then he arose and went out, and they accompanied him as
far as the door of the convent. And when they had
reached the door they said to him: "My lord, behold it is
a hundred and thirty years since this convent was built,
and there is none here who has seen this door since the
first [moment] she entered it, except this old woman who
has kept it now for an hundred and two years." They
said to him: "See! at this door we received thee, and at
this door we leave thee. But, my lord, go in peace to
thy retreat, and pray for us to thy Lord in thy monastery."
And when the blessed one went to the retreat, to the cell
which was in the wilderness, the sisters assembled themselves together and they stooped down and carried Saint
Onesima in their hands from the door of the convent to the
hall of service, rejoicing and triumphing about her as about
a precious treasure.

f. 91 a

And she was in the convent for about ten days. And whenever she went for a walk, they were gathering up the dust of her steps and rubbing it on their bodies as a medicament. And she was perplexed in her heart at the honour they were paying her. And she looked and saw that the door-keeper was not there; and she ran, and got out and went away, and no one knows where she went to; nor is even where she slept known to men.

And behold! the remembrance of her will be trans- f. 91 b mitted until the coming of the Son of God. To Him, and to His Father, and to the Holy Spirit, be praise, and honour, and adoration for ever. Here endeth the story of the blessed Onesima.

DRUSIS.

AGAIN, the martyrdom of Saint Drusis, and of those
who were martyred with her in Antioch, in the reign of
Trajan, the bad and wicked man. He had a daughter, a
child of his [own] body, but not of his [own] faith. This
Trajan had a burning desire and solicitude to build a
public bath in the city of Antioch in Syria, and all the
more because of his partners in wickedness, inasmuch as
both by name and by nature he was a tyrant.

He had also a sinful ardour and a great eagerness in
seeking to destroy and suppress the holy people of the
Christians. Therefore he was considering and imagining
evil things every day against the worshippers of the Christ.
And when he had put three people to death every day, he
went to see the work of the building of his public bath; for
he would not go previously to look at it until he had put
many Christians to death: the corpses of the saints lying
unburied in various places.

f. 92 a Now there were five virgin-nuns, three of them being
virgins and sisters and also their mother. And they
had a spiritual sister who was named Sufu. These lived
in a convent, and they went out by night and stole the
bodies of the saints who had been slain by the wicked
Trajan. And they wrapped them up and hid them in the
garden of their convent, anointing their limbs with sweet
ointment. But this matter was made known to the wicked
Trajan; that women were coming by night and stealing
the corpses of these unclean Christians. And if they were
permitted to act thus, every one would be driven from

the house of the gods, through the function of services to their corpses. And when the lamb of the Christ, Drusis, heard what had been said by her father about these people, she was moved to penitence in her spirit, and she stole a costly and valuable garment belonging to her father, and she ran away whilst the men of her body-guard were sunk in sleep; and when she went out, she saw these sister-nuns carrying the corpses of these holy martyrs, and she went with them into their convent, she also carrying a corpse on her pure back; rejoicing and exulting because of the good [fortune] that Sufu had received her amongst them.

But Adrianus was the adviser of the Emperor Trajan, f. 92 b and was also the betrothed bridegroom of the maiden Drusina; and he advised Trajan, saying, "My Lord the Emperor, command the soldiers to guard the city by night, that we may know who these are who steal the bones of the Christians who have met with a violent death." And this counsel was pleasing in the eyes of Trajan, and he himself gave orders to the soldiers, saying, "Watch and arrest for me those who steal the pestilent and unclean bones of these Christians, so that I may know because of what hope and expectation they do this."

Now whilst the soldiers were doing what they had been commanded by the Emperor [to do,] they found these five nuns with Drusina, who were accompanying and wrapping up the bodies of the saints, and they imprisoned these five carefully and put irons on their feet. Then they came to Drusis, and when they saw her, they said to each other, "Let us not put irons on this one, lest he take pity, like a father, on his daughter, and lay evil things upon us. But, nevertheless, let us be careful with her, and keep her till the morning."

And when the morning came, they made it known to

Trajan, saying, "My Lord the Emperor, the gods have fulfilled thy desire; but one thing prevents and restrains us from speaking in thy presence." Then he said to them, "Fear not." Then the soldiers of the wicked (Emperor) replied to him, saying: "We found five nuns whose faces were shining like the stars of heaven, and we imprisoned these nuns and put them in irons. But when we were going to lay hands on the sixth, we saw her face shining and beaming more than the sun; and on her therefore we did not dare to put irons; lest haply thy divinity should be angry with us. For she is our mistress, the daughter of the Emperor." Now when Trajan and his son-in-law Adrianus heard this they were very angry and they said to the soldiers, "O what a cruel death ye shall die! My lady Drusis is in her bed-chamber, and how say ye that she is imprisoned outside?" And the Emperor summoned the body-guards of his daughter, and inquired from them where Drusis was. But they said to him, "O Lord the Emperor, our life and our death are in thy hands. Whilst we were sleeping, we did not know what became of her." Then Trajan was persuaded, and believed what the lictors had said to him. And Adrianus counselled along with the priests, the teachers of evil, saying, "How hast thou commanded that these five women should die?" Some of them were saying that they should be thrown into the river Orontes, and be drowned; and others were saying, "Nay, but shame them and put them in the pillory[1]."

Adrianus said: "My Lord the Emperor, behold! there is the public hall, and nothing is wanting but that we should set up its own foundry. Command therefore, my Lord the Emperor, that there be a great furnace, and let copper things be fused in it, so that when they are consumed in it, not a single bone of them may be visible."

---

[1] Literally "place of retribution."

And this counsel pleased every one, and he sent and summoned the smelters of statues, and said to them: " Prepare a furnace for yourselves, lofty in height, and throw these wicked women into it. And whilst ye are heating them, pour copper upon them, so that their floor and the copper may become one; and then arrange it and make from them the bottom of brass. I desire then that at the feast of the consecration of the public bath, in the high place which is called Apollonià I may do what will appease the gods." And he commanded that Drusina should be kept with great care, saying, "Perhaps she will repent of what she has formerly done. And what the gods have bestowed upon her I will repay to them instead of her. For the faith of the Christians is the strongest of all witchcrafts; and it is very difficult for those who are falling into it to change to another religion."

Then Adrianus was inciting him, saying, "As thy majesty has commanded, I will arrange these [women] in order in the furnaces of Apollonia, near [this]. Command therefore, my Lord the Emperor, that it be proclaimed this day." Then f. 94 a he decreed a law and commandment in all the town after this manner: "Men of Antioch, all ye who believe in the gods, prepare yourselves and go up with us in the beginning of the month of Tammuz. For I desire and am ready to celebrate the consecration of the public bath of Trajan along with that of Zeus, that is, [in] the temples of Zeus and of Apollo. All therefore who hated the Christ, and were worshippers of idols, go ye up with songs and choruses, and in dazzling white dresses with me to the consecration of the public bath." And every one therefore who went in to wash himself, when he opened the first door of the building, fell down instantly and gave up the ghost, so that no man was able to enter by that first door. Then they made known this matter to the wicked Trajan. And the priests of

vanities and servants of worthless idols said in his presence,
"O Emperor, these bones which have been melted in that
copper have removed the mercies of the gods. But command that there be second furnaces and thus shalt thou
purify the public bath."

And when these things had been so done, Adrianus
counselled that the first copper of the furnace should be set
up in the middle of this, and that they should place them
(the women) in the public bath for the scorn and contempt
of every one. Then there appeared to the wicked Trajan
f. 94 b in a dream five pure lambs feeding in a park, and the
shepherd who tended them answered and said to the bad
and wicked Trajan, "Those whom thou hast expected to
expose to scorn, the good and gentle Shepherd has snatched
them from thee, and has put them in that place to which
Drusina also is ready to enter without stain." And when
the wicked man awoke he was very angry, because that
after their death those handmaids of God would be
bringing shame to his conscience and to his counsels.
Then he commanded that there should be two furnaces,
and that they should be heated every day.

And when first he arose from his sleep he issued a
decree after this fashion: "Ye men of Galilee, ye who
worship the Crucified One, save yourselves from tortures,
and me also from troubles; and let each of you throw
himself into these furnaces. For every time that I do
something to diminish you, your God makes you to in-
crease greatly."

Now when this decree was ordained, the lamb of God,
Drusina, listened, and every one of the Christians came,
and, with the loving fervour of faith, threw himself into the
furnace, whilst the Lord wrought miracles and wonders by
their means. But the simple lamb Drusina threw her glance

up towards heaven, and said: "O Lord God, if Thou hast willed the salvation of Thy handmaiden, chase away from me the vain fear of Trajan's threats. Receive me f. 95 a also in Thine espousals, and deliver me from wedlock with the wicked Adrianus. And plunge my custodians in sleep, and deliver me from them." And she took off the imperial robe and ran away with the intention of throwing herself into one of the furnaces with those who believed in the Christ. And when she came and stood beside the first furnace in the vicinity of the public bath of her father Trajan, she came to herself and said, "Behold! Drusina is going to God's presence, and she has no wedding garment. How shall I who have received no purification go to that Holy One? How shall I go, being unbaptized? I will go towards the second furnace. Perhaps one of God's servants will be found and he will baptize me and I shall go adorned as a bride." And when she came near to the second furnace, she saw all those who had thrown themselves [into it] for the sake of the Christ, and it grieved her much. And she saw a well of water to the north of the second furnace; and she lifted up her eyes[1] to heaven and said: "King of all kings, behold for Thy sake I have left my imperial palace, so that Thou mayest place me amongst the doorkeepers of Thy kingdom. Thou art pure and holy......look on me and baptize me by the Holy Spirit. Come therefore, Thou beloved Son, with the blessed and immortal Father, in thy Holy life-giving f. 95 b Spirit, and baptize me in this place, and let all the holy angels say Amen."

And when she had said, Amen, she took sweet salve and promptly anointed her whole body, and threw herself into the well. And thus was the holy Drusina crowned.

---

[1] Literally 'glance.'

But she lived for seven days after her immersion in the font, when she had partaken of the body and blood of our Lord Jesus the Christ from the hands of the holy angels. And on the eighth day she died[1] by being burnt in the furnace with those believers, and surrendered her spirit, to the glory of God the Father, and our Lord Jesus the Christ, to whom be praise and honour for ever.

Here endeth the story of Drusina, and of those who were martyred with her.

[1] Literally "was crowned."

BARBARA.

AGAIN the story of Saint Barbara in Heliopolis.
During the reign of the bad and wicked Aximus, there
was a governor [named] Aquinus, and there was a great
persecution of the Christians. And there was a certain
man in an Eastern land, in the city which is called Heliopolis,
and he lived in a village named Glasius, which is twelve
miles distant from Euchaita, and his name was Dioscurus;
and he was very rich, and he was benevolent, and he had
an only daughter, and her name was Barbara. And her
father made a high tower for her, and shut her up in it, so
that she might not be seen of men, because of the exceeding
fairness of her beauty. But some of the great and distinguished men of the city came to the father of Saint Barbara,
and tried to persuade him about a marriage union. But
when these things were spoken of to her father, he went
up to the tower beside his daughter, and said to her: "My
daughter, some great people have been trying to persuade
me concerning thee, to betroth thee to them. What dost
thou wish, my beloved daughter?" But she gazed on him
with anger, and lifted up her glance to heaven and said:
"Do not force me to do this, father, or else I will kill
myself."

Then he left her and went down. And he was solicitous
about the edifice which he was building to make it a
bath-house. And he set on a great number of workmen
so that they might finish his great building quickly; and
he commanded them that they should do it in a manner
suitable to what they were building, and then he gave

to each of them his full wage, and went to a far-off place. And he stayed there a good while.

And the handmaid of God, Barbara, went down to see that building, where the workmen were. And when she saw that great edifice, she saw two windows in the south side placed separately, and she said to the workmen, "Why have you put only two windows?" And they said to her, "Thus hath thy father commanded us." The handmaid of God, Barbara, said to them, "Do this thing that I command you, without fear. Set up another one for me." But they said to her, "We are afraid, lady, lest when thy father comes, he will be angry at us."

The handmaid of the Christ, Barbara, said to them, "I have told you, Do without fear what I tell you. And I will persuade my father concerning this." And they agreed to it, and set up another window as she had told them.

Now when the handmaid of God, Barbara, had walked into the bath-house, which was being built, she entered on its eastern side. And she drew with her finger on the marble wall the sign of the cross. And the figure of the cross is there till this day, for the penitence and confusion of those who see it and do not believe; whilst it was a cause of fear to all those who approached and entered it and believed, receiving healing and help.

And whilst this bath-house was a healing and a cure for all pains and sufferings, by means of that......which the saint of God brought into it: and when she had ascended to the tower in which she dwelt, she lifted up her eyes and saw those idols which her father worshipped. And she cried to the Holy and life-giving Spirit, and she conquered the Devil and spat in the faces of the idols, saying to them, "Your makers are like you, and all those who trust in you." And she climbed up to her tower and prayed continually to the Holy Cross.

f. 96 b

f. 97 a

Ps. cxv. 8

And when the work of the artificers was completely finished, her father arrived. But when he saw three windows set up, he said to the artificers: "Why have ye set up three windows?" And they said to him: "Thy daughter has commanded us to do thus." And he said to his daughter: "Hast thou commanded them to do thus?" And she said to him: "Yes, for I did well in commanding it; because it is pleasing that the Trinity enlightens all men who come into the world. For two would have been darkness."

And her father led her, and went down from the tower to the bath-house which he had built, and he said to her: "Tell me, in what way is the light of three better than that of two?" And the handmaid of God, Barbara, said to him: "Look and see! lo, there is the Father, and the Son, and the Holy Ghost."

Then her father was filled with rage, and drew his sword to strike her, and the holy Barbara prayed: and immediately the rock was cleft, and it received her inside of it[self] and it put her out on the mountain.

Now there were in that mountain two shepherds feeding [their] flocks, and they saw her running. But her father climbed to that mountain, and asked the shepherds about her. And one of them wishing to rescue her, denied with oaths f. 97 b that he had seen her, whilst the other shepherd pointed her out with his finger, and the handmaid of God, Barbara, cursed him. And immediately his flocks........and they are beside the tomb of the saint until this day. But as her father climbed up and found her, he dragged her by the hair of her head, and drove her with blows from the mountain, and he made her go into a little narrow cell and imprisoned her, and shut the door in her face and sealed it with his signet-ring, and set sentinels to guard her, so that no one might be able to open [it] to her until he should go and make her stand before Marcianus the governor; and should commit her to him for judgment.

And when the governor had arrived he commanded them to bring her. Then her father went in with Gerontius the prison-clerk, and they brought her out of the cell, and delivered her up to the governor, her father swearing to him by his gods that he would put her to death by severe punishments and bitter tortures.

Then the governor sat on his judgment-seat, and when he saw her beauty he said to her: " What dost thou wish? have pity on thy body and sacrifice, or else I will deliver thee up to bitter torments." The handmaid of God, Barbara, answered and said to him: "I am ready to offer the sacrifice of praise to the Saviour of my soul, to Him who hath made the heavens and the earth, and the sea, and all that in them is; for concerning thy gods the prophet David has said: 'They have a mouth, but they speak not; they have eyes but they see not; they have ears, but they hear not; they have hands, but they feel not; they have feet, but they walk not, and they cry not with their throats. Their makers are like unto them, and so are all those who trust in them.' "

Then the governor was filled with rage and anger; and he commanded them to strip the holy woman, and to tear her body with an ox-hide, and to rub her wounds with a hairy garment, so that all her body should be bathed in her blood. And he commanded them to take her to the prison-house, until he should consider by what punishment he would put her to death.

And at midnight a great light dawned upon her, and our Redeemer appeared to her, saying, " Be strong and of good courage, my beloved martyr; there is great joy about thee in heaven and on earth, because of thy witness. Be not afraid of the threats of the tyrant, for I am with thee,

f. 98 a

Ps. cxv. 5

and I will deliver thee from all the punishments that they may bring upon thee." And immediately her wounds were healed, and not one of them appeared on her body. And when the Lord had said these things to her, He set His seal upon her and ascended to heaven with His holy angels. And the handmaid of the Christ rejoiced and was glad at the revelation of the Lord.

Now there was with her a certain woman who feared God, whose name was Juliana, and she had joined herself to the holy Barbara, and she saw the wonders and the signs f. 98 b that God did by the hands of the holy one, and she gave herself up along with her to stripes and to tortures. And at the dawn of the day the governor commanded them to bring her. And when he saw her wounds that they were healed and had disappeared, he said to her, " I see, Barbara, how the gods care about thee, and they love thee, and heal (thee), for lo! they have even healed thy wounds." The martyr of the Christ, Barbara, answered and said to the governor, " In truth thou hast gods which are blind and dumb and stupid, and that cannot move. How can they heal wounds—they who can neither cure themselves nor help themselves? But nevertheless He who has cured me is our Lord Jesus the Christ, the Redeemer of the world, the Son of the Living God ; He whom thou art unworthy to behold because of the blind remoteness[1] of thy heart, which is blinded by the devil."

Then the governor was enraged and ground his teeth like a lion ; and he commanded them to tear her sides with a comb and singe them with burning lamps, and to strike her on the crown of her head with a hammer.

But when Juliana, she who loved God, saw the blows that they had arranged, she wept convulsively. Then said Marcianus the governor, " Who is this woman ? " Those

---

[1] Literally " blindness of the remoteness."

f. 99 a who were standing in his presence said to him, "She is a Christian, and is grieved about Barbara." And the governor was enraged, and commanded them to hang her up, and to tear her sides with combs, and to singe all her body with lamps. But the holy Barbara lifted up her eyes to heaven and said : "Thou, Lord Jesus the Christ, knowest what is in the hearts of those who love Thee. Forsake me not, thine handmaid, nor my sister Juliana."

When they had bravely endured these tortures, the governor commanded that the breasts of the holy Barbara should be cut off with knives. And whilst they were being cut off, the martyr of the Christ, Barbara, was singing psalms and saying : "Lord, turn not Thy face away from us, and take not Thy Holy Spirit from Thy handmaid, but turn to me the joy of Thy salvation, and may Thy glorious Spirit uphold me in Thy fear."

And while they were bearing these punishments bravely, the governor commanded that they should separate Juliana from the saint, in the prison, and guard her. But about the holy Barbara he commanded that they should lead her about naked through all that province and should beat her unmercifully with stripes.

But the martyr of the Christ, Barbara, looked up to heaven, and said, "O God, who dost cover the sun with clouds, let down upon me the wing of Thy mercy, and be my helper; and cover this my naked body, and let it not be seen by these bad and wicked men." Whilst she was saying this the Lord came, seated on the chariot of cherubim; and He sent the angels and clothed her with a white

f. 99 b garment. And whilst they were leading her about in all that province, they brought her to a certain village which was called Dalisin, to the governor Marcianus. Then that governor commanded that she should die by the sword, with her sister Juliana.

The father of the saint was thereafter filled with rage, and took her away from the governor, and led the holy Barbara up to a mountain. She was eager and hastened, so that she might attain to the complete reward from above to which she was called along with the holy Juliana. And whilst the holy Barbara was on the way she prayed and said : "O Lord Jesus the Christ! co-eternal with the Father, the invisible, the uncreated, the crown of martyrs, He who has stretched out and laid the foundations of the earth; He who commands the clouds and they produce the rain, and brings down His dew on the good and on the bad : He who walketh on the back of the sea and does not wet His steps, for all obey Thee, Lord Jesus the Christ, because they are the work of Thy hands. Do thou grant us the request which I seek from Thee, and give grace to me, Thy handmaid. And to every one who makes mention of Thy holy name, and of the name of Thy handmaid, and who makes a commemoration and remembers my martyrdom : O Lord God my Saviour, let no plague of infection nor of cancer come upon that country nor on that house, on the body of any one who is in it, whether male or female, nor yet upon the children. f. 100 a And remember not against them their sins, but grant a recovery even to the lepers. For Thou knowest, O Lord! that they are flesh and blood, the work of Thy pure and holy hands. And to Thee honour and adoration is due for ever and ever. Amen."

And when she had said Amen, there was a voice from heaven near her saying, "Come, my martyr, thou art clothed with suffering, and thou hast won the victory in thine own person. Come, rest in the mansions of my Paradise, in Heaven, with my beloved Juliana. For what thou hast asked hath been given to thee. And all those who are seized with the diseases which thou hast mentioned will be healed, whilst they confess their sins."

And when the martyr of the Christ, Barbara, had heard these things, she went to the place which was prepared for her to die in it. And she was crowned by the sword of her father Dioscurus. And she died, the holy virgin-martyr Barbara, with Juliana, she who had attached herself to her. And their heads were cut off in the...indiction, in that place.

But when the father of the holy Barbara came down from the mountain, fire fell from heaven and consumed him and Marcianus the governor, so that it was seen also by those who stood round them.

The holy Barbara was crowned in the month of December on Thursday.

Glory and honour be to God for ever and ever.

Here endeth the martyrdom of the holy Barbara.

MARY.

AGAIN, the martyrdom of the blessed Mary.

Hadrian and Antoninus, the wicked Emperors, had sent an Imperial decree, that everyone who worshipped the Christ should turn to their own religion and law, whilst they [who] should eat of the impure sacrifices should live and not die ; and that those who should be contentious and should resist the decree were to be delivered over to judgment.

Now at that time the blessed Mary, the bride of the Christ, had grown up in the Christian confession ; for she was the bond-servant of Tertullius, a chief man of the city. But she was altogether a free woman of the Christ, and as it is written, " He who is called being a slave in the Christ, is the Lord's freeman."

Now the birthday of the son of Tertullius arrived. And on that day he offered sacrifices and libations to the demons. And the noble Mary was slandered in the presence of her mistress by one of her companions. And she called her and said to her, " Tell me, why didst thou fast, and didst not keep[1] the feast with us ? Was it a vexation to thee ? "

Mary said, " Because I have lately been fasting. Or didst thou not know that I am a Christian, like my fathers?"

And her mistress constrained her by force to eat. But she cried to the heavenly Bridegroom, to Jesus the Christ. And she answered and said, " Ye have power over this my body, but not over my soul. Let my speech be heard (though spoken) with boldness. Dost thou not understand that the festival of thy son was celebrated with the music of

---

[1] Literally "make."

flutes and with cymbals and with impure rites and with drums and with lyres? But the festival of the Christians is celebrated with fasting and with praying and with purity and with spiritual songs."

But as her mistress could not endure her boldness, she said, "I will treat thee so that thou shalt die of scourging." Mary answered, saying, "Do what thou wilt, because of the help of the Lord that is with me." And when her husband Tertullius came from the Forum she told him about the blessed Mary. And immediately without examination he commanded them to scourge her with whips. And he commanded them further to shut her up alone in a closet, and to give her food by measure. But the blessed one praised God, praying continually, that she might remain constant in bearing testimony for the Christ.

And when three days[1] had passed it was told to the governor of the city that Tertullius had a certain Christian maid-servant in his house, and he was entreated that they might be in their city without any danger till the matter should be inquired into. And on the following day the governor sat on the judgment-seat, and commanded that they should fetch Tertullius. And all the Prætorium was assembled and all the people of the city. And the law of the Emperors was read in their presence, in which it was thus written: "The great and mighty Emperors, the terrible and merciful Diocletian and Antoninus, the saviours and architects and supporters of the whole inhabited world, to all those who are under the sway[2] of our Empire, and observe the right of our majesty and are diligent in the worship of the gods, much greeting.

"Forasmuch as a report has come to our ears, that suddenly the teachings of various men have sprung up,

f. 101 b

---

[1] Sinai Palimpsest "months."
[2] Literally "hand," literally "mercifulness."

which are contrary to the commandments of the gods and that seek to abolish the festivals of sacrifice, and the former laws of our ancestors and their great festivals are derided, therefore with the advice of the two Emperors, we command simultaneously, because we desire that all men should worship with reverence[1] and fear, and should propitiate the gods by sacrifice, and should not be like wandering beasts. And whosoever shall hide a Christian man or Christian woman, young men or maidens, old men or children, he shall die by the edge of the sword ; and his wealth shall be given to the treasury. And whosoever shall trace out these people, he shall receive all that they possess, and four hundred dinars shall be given to him over and above by the Emperors. And if a man be found who has transgressed these things which we command, he shall be held guilty by the law."

And after the decree of the Emperors had been read, the governor answered and said to Tertullius, " Make a reply concerning this matter, for this is not a simple calamity for thee."

The advocate, who stood up, said, " Hear us, O wise judge. The girl in whose account this innocent man is accused, was given with the dowry of his wife."

The governor said, " Is his wife of a free family ? " f. 102 a The advocate replied, " Yes, my lord, she is the daughter of a certain Aquilinus." The governor said, " Was this girl born in the house or was she bought with money ? " Tertullius said, " She was born in the house, but her parents were bought by sale." Then the governor asked, " Is the steward alive or dead ? " Tertullius said, " Yes, my lord, he is dead." Then he asked him, " Are the parents of the girl alive ? " Tertullius said, " They are not alive." The governor said, " Were they of the religion of the Christians, or did they fear the gods ? " The master of the

---

[1] Literally, "mercifulness."

girl answered, "They also worshipped the Christ who was crucified."

The advocate said, "O most wise of judges, they have scourged her with many stripes, that she might come to this worship; and if not, thou canst not turn her by force from her faith."

And when the governor had asked all these things he said, "Because the whole of the Pretorium bears witness to Tertullius, and they do honour to his family with their praises, because he is of the senate, and they proclaim what is straightforward and good about him, and that he is a worshipper of the gods, and obedient to the Emperors; and I also am convinced by the ancient writings, and the innocency of the man has been truly shown to me, he is therefore freed from our judgment until the Emperors can hear him: but let the insolent girl stand before the judgment-seat." And the lictors brought the bride of the Christ and placed her before the judge in the court of judgment. Then the wicked and bloodthirsty people shouted against her (saying) that she ought to be burnt alive. But the thoughts of the believing woman were all with God, and she looked up to the height of heaven, and called with boldness on our Lord, saying:

f. 102 b

"O Lord Jesus the Christ, Son of the Living God, true Son of the Father, whose birth no man can oppose; neither emperors, nor judges, nor yet principalities, nor powers, nor yet lords, nor yet cherubim, nor yet seraphim; because, O Lord, they all have been created by Thy hands; and without Thy mandate nothing could have existed; and only Thy Father knoweth thee. Therefore He sent Thee from the highest heavens to the sinners who were awaiting Thee. Thou, O Lord the Christ, art the glorious High-Priest, the Redeemer and Saviour of our souls. O Lord, help Thy handmaiden, for she has no helper but Thee; that Thy holy name may be glorified, whilst Thou doest these things quickly. Accept the prayer of thy handmaid."

The governor was amazed and astonished for about an hour: and he commanded that they should bring her before the judgment-seat; and he asked her, saying, "What is thy name?" And she returned an answer, saying, "Why dost thou seek after my name? I am a Christian." The governor said, "Is he who stands [there] thy master?" The noble woman said, "He is the master of my body only, but over my soul God rules."

The governor said, "Why dost thou not worship the f. 103 a gods as thy master worships (them)?" Mary said, "I am a Christian, and I do not worship the dumb idols, but I worship the living and true God, who is eternal."

The judge said, "From whom didst thou receive (the idea) of being a Christian?" Mary said, "I received it from my parents." The judge said, "And were thy parents Christians?" Mary said, "They also received it from their parents." The judge said, "I suppose that before they received it ye were chiefs in this religion. But even if it be-so, approach and sacrifice, so that thy master may be quit of the accusation of the law." The noble woman said, "How has this entered into the desire of my mind? He also ofttimes constrained me to eat of what was sacrificed, and has tortured me with many scourgings, but the love of the Christ my master is stronger in grace, more than the torments of the wicked (man). And because my parents laid hold of the divine teaching which was preached by Paul the Apostle, Rom. viii. for he said, 'Who shall separate us from the love of the 35 Christ? shall tribulation, or anguish, or persecution, or nakedness, or the sword?' And because they laid hold of these things, they confessed the Christ, and believed that neither death, nor life, nor angels, nor principalities, nor

f. 103 b things present, nor any other creature can separate us from the love of God, which is in Jesus Christ our Lord. As I also say the truth, and I lie not, my conscience, which is Christ, bearing me witness, that I depart from this world a Christian." Mary said, "Will thy torturers continue to the end, as they have but a short time? Therefore do what thou wilt, for I have the Christ, the Saviour of my soul."

And when the judge had heard this he commanded that they should strip her and prepare her for the tortures. And when many people saw her, they wept bitterly and shed tears with sobs, and they cried out against the governor, saying that he should show her a little patience. But the governor was not willing to be persuaded, but decreed that they should torture the blessed one. And again the bystanders cried out against the governor, "Thou judgest wickedly; thou art going beyond the law."

And when the governor heard the voice he was astonished. It appeared to him that it was not only men who were crying, but also the buildings were wailing. And he commanded the lictors who were standing there not to keep her. And he said to the people who were present, "Wherefore are ye making a tumult, and resisting the commands of the Emperors? Is it not right for us to hearken unto the commands of the Emperors?"

They all answered as with one mouth, saying, "The judges of the province, the victorious Emperors, command

f. 104 a with gentleness and persuasiveness that men should be led forward to sacrifice. But if they do not obey, they are to die by the sword. Now if she does not obey, command concerning her that she die by the sword. And we request this, that three days be given to her, so that perhaps she may be persuaded, and fulfil the law of the Emperors." The judge said, "Do ye persuade her, for, lo! ye have

seen that she was not in the least persuaded by me."
The interpreter said, "What dost thou say, Mary, if three
days be given to thee, wilt thou sacrifice?"

Mary answered, "My helper from of old was the Lord."
The judge said, "I give thee a respite of three days, and
I swear by all the gods that if thou art so stubborn again
thou shalt die by a variety of tortures." The noble woman
said, "Only one thing do I ask of thee, that my master
shall be held blameless, and shall be liberated, as innocent,
from the judgment." The governor said, "He shall be
liberated blameless; and thou, if thou wilt be persuaded,
shalt receive gifts, and shalt find freedom, which is a great
thing among men." Mary said, "As the Christ liveth,
He who hath given me all freedom, and in whom I trust."

Then he commanded that she should be kept carefully
without dishonour. And the blessed one descended
from [before] the tribunal and signed herself with purity.
And she ran actively and lifted up her eyes to
Ps. cxxi. 1 heaven and prayed, saying, "I will lift up mine eyes
unto the mountains, from whence my helper shall come.
My help cometh from before the Lord, who made
heaven and earth." And suddenly she saw wonderful f. 104 b
things; the heavens which were opened and troops of the
angels and the archangels standing, and the prophets, and
the apostles, and the martyrs, and the confessors, and
amongst them she saw Thekla her sister. And then she
saw the cherubim and the seraphim and the Son of God
on the right hand of His Father. And thus the noble
woman rejoiced, as one who has just entered through the
gate of Paradise. But as for her persecutors their limbs
became weak, and they fell, because of the help of the
Lord, which accompanied His handmaiden. But many
others were pursuing her. And when they surrounded
her on every side she cried with a loud voice, saying,
"Lord Jesus the Christ, Thou art He who came down to

the fiery furnace in Babylon and rescued the three young men from the fire. And Thou art He who didst shut the mouth of the lions and rescued Daniel Thy servant, and didst lift him out of the lions' den unharmed. Also Thou didst deliver Jonah from the sea and from the belly of the fish, and Thou didst bring him up in three days. Thou, Lord Jesus, didst give light to the blind, and didst give hearing to the deaf. Thou wast the Healer of all sufferers, and the expectation of all the righteous. Thou art He, Lord, who didst hear the voice of the blood of Abel, and didst avenge him of Cain his brother. Thou art He, Lord, who wast present with Joseph, and didst deliver him from being slain by his brothers. Thou art He, Lord, who didst come, and art about to come to judge the quick and the dead. Redeemer of Thy handmaid! Jesus the Christ! hearken to my voice, and receive my soul; for dogs have compassed me about. Deliver not Thine handmaid into the hands of those who hate Thee. Thou, Lord, art the Mediator between God and man. Hear, Lord, the voice of Thy handmaiden, and redeem me according to the plenteousness of Thy mercy."

And when she had finished her prayer, the rock before her was cleft, and it opened its bosom for [her] deliverance f. 105 a like a foster-mother for her son; and it treasured up the bride of the Christ in its bosom. And the great crowd who were there went round about like blind people seeking for her. And when they came to that rock they found on the top of it something like three finger-breadths of the corner of her veil, and the fringes which were visible. And they returned and informed the governor of what had happened.

And the governor, in a great rage, commanded a certain man whose name was Placimus, the ruler of the city, to go to that place with a great many people, and to quarry the rock, and to dig deep in the earth, until they

should find the blessed one. And when Placimus had
received this commandment, he ordered the herald to cry
aloud in the city and to say, " All ye citizens! assemble
yourselves, and gather at the appointed time, and come ;
and let us take vengeance for our goddess." And when
they were all assembled in the temple of the idols, he
commanded them to take iron tools that they might dig
the place with them. And when they were all assembled,
and were ready to go and work, suddenly there was lightning from the east, and fearful thunder, and a great earthquake, and there appeared two terrible horsemen descending
as it were from heaven to earth ; and their lances were like
burning lamps, and at the same moment many fell down
through fright and died. And those who remained were
chased by them as far as the door of the idol-temple. But
when Placimus arrived at the door he also suddenly fell and
died. And fire came down from heaven and burnt up the f. 105 b
house and the idols, and many of the wicked people were
burnt. And those who died were, with those who were
burnt, two thousand seven hundred in number. And those
who were left fled to the city, and they cried, saying, " Great
is Mary's God and great is the God of the Christians, and
He is God in truth."

And they ran in a crowd and went into the church,
seeking mercy from God, for the wicked things which they
had done, And three thousand souls from amongst them
believed on that day. And in the days of the martyrdom of
the blessed Mary the persecution of the Christians ceased[1].

Here endeth the martyrdom of the blessed and noble
Mary, and she conquered in the conflict with the wicked
judge.

---

[1] The Sinai Palimpsest adds: " May the Lord grant to us to find mercy
in the judgment, in the place where there shall be a recompence to the
righteous, (and) shame to the sinners, by the grace and mercy of our Lord
Jesus the Christ. With Him also to His Father be glory and honour with the
Holy Ghost for ever."

IRENE.

AGAIN, the story of Saint Irene.

In the six hundredth and twenty-first year of the reign of Licinius, king of the city of Magedo, an only daughter was born to him, and he called her name Penelope. And when she was six years old her father and mother consulted as to how they should shut her up, and in what place there should be a retreat where she might learn [her] letters, until she should come to full stature and arrive at a marriageable age, so that the wedding-feast might take place when she should emerge from the retreat. And they proposed to build a castle outside of the city and to surround it with a strong wall; and that Apellianus, her secretary, should mount with ropes by means of the contrivances of an engine of the artificers to her own high window in the castle; and whilst he sat outside there were curtains hung between him and the maiden, [and] he was to teach her letters. Licinius the king agreed on these things with his wife. And they began at once to the work, and he commanded and the artificers came, and he set the men to work immediately. And he appointed three hundred overseers who made the slaves and the builders work. And five thousand skilful carpenters to prepare wooden in-struments, and two thousand stone-cutters, men who were to cut stones from the mountain, and three thousand carts which were to carry the stones. For the king was eager and hurried the workmen to finish the castle in nine months.

But when they had begun the work, the building progressed chiefly through the insistence of the king who was beside them. And when the castle was completed, with its ornamentation, and its beauty, and everything suitable to it, the king desired to have a dedication festival for it; and he sent and invited five neighbour kings, and they came at the appointed time with their armies, and with a great endless crowd accompanying them.

And when the king saw the great crowd, he commanded f. 106 b that five thousand oxen should be slaughtered, and ten thousand sheep; and these kings and their armies enjoyed themselves for thirty days; and at the end of three days every man departed to his home. And the kings and their armies went one by one to his city.

But afterwards the king called for his daughter and said to her, affectionately, " My daughter, I have built a castle for thee, adorned with all beautiful things; elegant in its loveliness, very wonderful in its aspect, glorious in its appearance, firm in its foundations, and strong in its walls, and superb in its apartments, loftier than all work, an astonishment to its beholders; wonderful in its construction, impregnable and invincible to men, that cannot be over-thrown by giants. Now therefore, my beloved daughter, I wish to shut thee up there in that castle for a fixed term of years, until thou shalt come to full stature, and arrive at thy wedding-day. Do not murmur then, my daughter, and let there be no anxiety in thy heart, and let not fear dwell in thy mind. For, lo! I have commanded that ninety-eight gods shall mount thither with thee and take care of thee. For I will set up seven gods in each chamber of the castle, that the evil one and his power may not rule there, nor trouble thy childhood. Be not therefore anxious, for, lo! I have made everything that is beautiful for thy comfort: my beloved daughter."

But when the king's daughter heard these things from her father, she lifted up her voice with weeping, and said f. 107 a

to her father with bitter tears, "Thou art shutting me up
alive, my father, within the gates of Hades, whence I
shall never go out; and I shall never again hear the sweet
voice of my mother nor of other women. I shall not
see the sun, nor the moon, nor shall I contemplate the
brilliancy of heaven, nor the stars. My eye shall not
delight in the birds of the air, I shall not distinguish
between day and night in my prison-house whilst I am in
it. I shall raise my [voice] to heaven. Never again shall
I walk on the earth, I shall not even need a shoe, except
for ornament. Forasmuch as I cannot take a walk, what
can it profit me? Affliction and anxiety come upon me
from all sides. My father! I shall never again see children
like myself, of my own age. Henceforth I renounce all
created things. Forasmuch as I shall suffer in Hades and
in the grave, whence I shall never go out, truly my
beloved parents will weep for me with sobs and even with
lamentations."

And when she had said these things there was great
weeping and much mourning in the house of the king. And
also the faces of all his servants wore a look of sadness.

But when the queen, the mother of the girl, saw her
daughter, and heard these words from her, she rose in haste
and went hurriedly to the girl, and threw her arms round
her neck, and embraced her weeping. And she said to the
f. 107 b king with anxious tears, and with bitterness of heart,
"I shall not leave my daughter. I will go to the grave
with her and be imprisoned in Hades. I will die with her,
and I will live with her."

And it came to pass, on a certain day in the palace of
her father, that at the turn of the day the king dismissed
all those who were coming in and going out from his
presence; and he led his daughter and went to the castle
which he had built; he and his daughter and a great crowd

of the magnates of the city with him. And he took his daughter up to that castle and her thirteen handmaidens with her for her honour and for service. And he took up a throne and her chairs, and a dining-table and a candlestick; and all the vessels for her service with her; and her ornaments, and her trinkets, and her crowns, all of gold, and emeralds, and pearls; eleven changes of raiment of all colours; of linen, and silk, and purple. And afterwards the king and the queen kissed the girl and went out. And they left her in peace, they and the magnates of the city, whilst the slaves and the handmaidens were weeping like people who are mourning and grieving for a dead person at the grave.

Then the king commanded and they shut the outer doors of the castle and he sealed them with his signet ring, and he commanded that they were not to be opened until the time arrived for his daughter to be betrothed to a husband. But the king had made the castle as a pavilion because he feared lest the sun should look upon the girl's beauty and blacken her colour with its heat. And f. 108 a when he had shut the doors and sealed them he entered the city, and set guards over the castle outside its walls, one thousand five hundred men, that they might keep watch continually by day and by night.

But during all the days of her imprisonment Apellianus her secretary came to teach her letters. And the guards drew him up with the ropes of the machine to the highest window of the castle. And he sat outside and taught her letters, never seeing her face.

But the girl, the daughter of the king, meditated in the castle when she was six years old, and she was there six years and three months, and at the end of this period the king's daughter saw as in a dream that the window on the east side of the castle was opened, and she saw that a

dove entered from it carrying an olive-leaf in its mouth,
and it set it on the table in front of her bed and went
out. And afterwards she saw again an eagle entering by
the same window and carrying in its mouth a wreath
adorned with all flowers, and it also set it on that table
and went out. And she again saw a raven carrying a
wriggling serpent, and it set it upon the table and went
out. And she saw these things and called out for her
[confidante] and they took refuge with each other out of
fright.

But on the morning of the day her secretary came as
usual to teach her letters. And she related to him all the
f. 108 b signs and wonders which she had seen. Her teacher said
to her, "Do the objects which the birds of heaven laid upon
the table remain there until now?" But she said to him.
"No, we saw them only in the vision; and they were taken
away immediately from before my eyes." And the teacher
was filled with the inspiration[1] of the Spirit, and he said
to her: "Hearken, O daughter of the king! The dove
which thou hast seen is the doctrine of the teaching of the
Wisdom of God; and the olive-leaf is the grace of the
Christ, and it announces the opening of the baptismal font.
And the eagle is a great and powerful king, and the wreath
which it carried in its mouth, adorned with all flowers, is
the vocation which hath called thee to the espousals of the
Heavenly Bridegroom, and the perfection which is completed by faith. And the raven is Satan the weak and
crafty one, [who is] also the tempter[2] of the righteous; and
the serpent which he carried in his mouth is affliction and
anxiety, misery and tumult, and persecutions. Therefore
hearken, oh queen and daughter of the king! to what I
tell thee. Thou art called to the city of the great and
Heavenly King; and thou shalt be hidden under the
shadow of His wings. Thou shalt surely see much afflic-

---

[1] Literally "teaching."   [2] Literally "temptation."

tion upon earth. And thy father and thy mother shall deliver thee up to thine enemies; and thy father himself shall be a......and persecutor to thee; and shall meditate evil, and not good, against thee. But why do I talk much with thee? for, lo! a man of God shall be sent to thee, an f. 109 a angel of peace from the presence of the mighty King of Heaven, and he will teach thee all that is necessary to thee." And when her secretary had said these things to her, he descended from her presence at the time when he was accustomed to do so.

Now at the dawn of day the king said to the queen, "The day has arrived for the wedding-feast of our daughter. Let us go and see her face; for the day of the marriage is come."

And the king and queen arose and went both of them to the castle; and the king called his daughter. And she stooped down; and he saw that her face was shining and lovely like the radiance of the sun. Then he was filled with a great joy and said to his daughter, "My daughter, the day of thy wedding has arrived. Tell me therefore, my daughter, that I may tell[1] the time and the place to those who are entering and who are going out; and that I may appoint and make known the date of thy wedding-feast; and that one of the sons of a king who shall please thee, and shall enliven thy soul, let him be thy betrothed."

His daughter said to him, "My father, have patience with me for a single week[2], and I will take counsel with my thoughts; and then after the lapse of a week[2] I will tell thee."

And when the king had heard the speech of his daughter, he was persuaded by her, and said, "As thou wilt, my daughter, be it unto thee."

Then he left her and went into the town rejoicing and with exulting mind. Now after her father had left her and

---

[1] Literally "give."   [2] Literally "one week of days."

had gone into the city, she drew nigh and spoke to the gods—the idols—those which had been set up there beside her. And she curtsied before them, and said to them, "If ye be gods, hearken to my voice, [regarding] what I say to you. Give me back an answer and teach me the true

f. 109 b thing that will help. My father will constrain me to be given to an husband. But I have accustomed myself to the solitude of widowhood, and to the humility of sterility, and to the desolateness of orphanhood. Verily the wedding-feast of the world leadeth away from the truth and it is an obstacle in the presence of the Lord."

She said again to the idols, "If ye be gods, tell me beforehand. Shall I be given to a husband, or no?' And she saw that there was no voice, nor any one that listened, nor any who gave her an answer. And she turned herself to the eastern window and she looked at the sky, and she prayed and said, "Lord of the heaven and of the earth, and of the seas, and of all that creepeth in them, if Thou art God the Almighty, Jesus the Christ, the Son of the Living God, He whom the Galileans have preached, if it is proper for me to make a transitory wedding-feast for myself, and to be given to a mortal man, and a bride-groom who will perish ; show me plainly Thy divinity." And when she had said this she sang praises to God.

On that night she lifted up her eyes, and saw the angel of the God standing beside her, clothed in white. And when she saw him, she was sore afraid, and her mind was perturbed. And when the angel saw that she was afraid[1], he said to her, "Peace be unto thee, fear not, for behold ! thou hast found mercy and grace before God. And I have been sent to thee to show thee and to teach thee the things to come. And henceforth thy name shall no more be called Penelope, but Irene, which, being

f. 110 a interpreted, is Peace. And thou shalt be a strong tower

---

[1] Literally "that fear had fallen upon her."

against all the tricks of the crafty one; and many men shall find a refuge with thee, and shall repent and believe in God for thy sake; a thousand three hundred and thirty thousand people, men, women and children. And everything that Apellianus thy teacher has said to thee he said well, about those birds which thou hast seen, and what they carried and laid upon thy table. He spoke justly, for the Holy Spirit spake by him and prophesied, and that man is not far from the kingdom of God. For a man of God shall come to thee from Paul the Apostle, a skilful doctor of the church of God. And he shall have a letter on (his person) and he will read it in thy presence, and will teach thee the faith and the religion of God; and he will baptize thee in the name of the Father, and the Son, and the Holy Ghost. Surely an angel of God will accompany him, and will break down the castle, and he will enter thy presence and baptize thee in the name of the Father, and the Son, and the Holy Ghost. And after thy baptism power and strength will be given to thee, with fortitude and the wisdom of God. And thou shalt have purity from guilt, with the remission of sins."

And the angel went up from her to heaven. And afterwards the blessed lamb of the Christ remained rejoicing and exulting in her mind and praising God for all that she had heard from the angel. And she was looking for the arrival of Timothy that she might be baptized by him, and might receive the sign of the Christ. And on the following day there came to her the holy priest Timothy, accompanied by an angel of God, and said to her, "What is thy care, my daughter, [because of which] f. 110 b I am come to thee to-day?"

And she said, "It is well that thou art come, my father and lord, for it is the time that my sins should be remitted, and my transgressions and faults should be blotted out by thy coming, in peace, and that I should obtain salvation in God." And when the holy priest Timothy had heard these words he gave thanks, and blessed the oil and the water; and he baptized her in the name of the Father, and the Son, and the Holy Ghost; her, and the thirteen handmaidens who were with her, whom her father had given to her for her service. And after she and her handmaidens had been baptized that holy priest taught them the faith and the fear of God. And the angel who was with him was taken away.

And the blessed lamb of the Christ blessed and praised God without ceasing. And she turned to those senseless idols of the gods and said to them, "I entreated and besought you to tell me the truth, and ye did not tell me. Now therefore, if ye are gods, stand up for yourselves. Jer. x. 11 For the gods who did not make the heaven and the earth shall perish from beneath the heaven." And she obtained power and strength and heroism. And she lifted these idols with power, and flung them from the eastern window, f. 111 a to the ground below, saying to them, "Stand up yourselves, if you can, and help yourselves by your own power, for ye were not able to do anything to help me."

But they were greatly smashed by [their] fall from the great height, and they were ground to pieces like salt, and became as dust.

But when the appointed period of seven days had come to an end the king Licinius went to the castle to see his daughter. And he called her and said to her, "My daughter, behold the appointed period of seven days is finished, as thou didst say, according to thy wish, and what dost thou say?"

Then all the great men who were with him said to him, "O king, mayst thou live for ever! Let thy majesty command and bring down the maiden from the castle, and bring her into the city, and there will we delight ourselves with her beauty ; and she shall be in the palace of the king."

Then when she had heard [it], she said, "After I have entered the palace of the Heavenly King and have dwelt in it ; and have delighted in the seal and in the espousals of Jesus the Christ, the Son of the Living God, shall I leave Him and enter a palace of human weeping and full of sin ? " " Be it far from thee," said the nobles to her. " From what thou speakest perhaps thou art a Christian ? " She said to them, " Now you certainly know that I am the handmaid of the Christ and the bride of Jesus. For behold all the week that I was baptized these were the days of my wedding-feast and of the joy of my nuptials. Oh! do ye not see the destruction of your gods, and if they did not help themselves when they were hurled down from above, how can they help you ? Truly ye cherish a vain and empty f. 111 b hope in them. For all the gold and silver that ye possess, which ought to be given to the orphans, and to the widows, and to the needy, and to the oppressed in spirit, ye have called for the goldsmiths, and have given it to them ; and by their skill they have made you artificial gods ; and ye have worshipped them, and have given to unsavoury demons and to dead idols the adoration which was due to God. They have eyes, but they see not; they have ears, Ps. cxv. 5 but they hear not; and there is no breath in their mouth. They that make them shall be like unto them, and every one that trusteth in them. Therefore ye are the oppressors of the orphans and of the widows, and spoilers of the poor and of the unfortunate ; and the enemies of righteousness; and aliens from God ; fornicators and adulterers ; deceivers and deniers of God. Repent and turn to the living God. Know ye the merciful God who is able to kill and to make alive; to bring [down] to Sheol and to bring up

[again]. Turn ye to God, while there is room, before the day
of doom cometh, and ye fall into the judgment of righteousness. Hearken to me, my own father, for my word is to
thee! know what I say to thee. When thou didst begin
to build this castle, thou didst build it with many people
—there was no end to them—and by thy presence which
was with them at every moment. Thou didst finish it in
nine months, with its ornaments and with all its de-
corations; and thou wert praised amongst men and lauded
for thy work. But our adored God made the heaven and
the earth and the seas, and all that moveth in them in six
f. 112 a days; He made the sun and the moon and the stars, and to
all of them He gave names. He created the mountains
and the hills and the valleys and the plains. He created
every tree whose seed[1] is in itself on the earth. And on
the completion of these things He formed man in His own
image and in His likeness; and clothed him with brightness
and made him lord and ruler over all the brutes and the
beasts, and the creeping things and the flying things, and
subjected all these creatures to Him; and He created them[2]
all by His word; and that was our Lord Jesus the Christ;
He whom the Jews have crucified; He who has been
persecuted by the unjust people, and He was taken, and
was scourged, and was crowned with a crown of thorns,
and was crucified, and He tasted the vinegar and the gall
on the cross; which sweetened our bitterness; He died
and was buried; and in three days He rose by the Divine
power which dwelt in Him. And He was exalted and
taken up to Heaven to His Father. And He sat down on
the right hand of Him who sent Him. And the cherubim
bear His throne, and the seraphim stand before Him, and
He is worshipped by the hosts of Heaven. He it was

[1] Or "power of germinating," see Gen. i. 29.
[2] Literally "all these creatures."

who in six days created and made everything by His word. This light hath dawned on the earth, and those who are sitting in darkness and in the shadow of death have seen His light. And the truth ran upon the earth; the sick were healed; the afflicted were comforted; even the diseased were cured; the lepers were cleansed; the demons were cast out; the palsied were made whole; the [eyes of the] blind were opened; and the dead were raised up; and souls were saved and the lost were found; f. 112 b and the erring turned back; and the sinners repented; and the righteous rejoiced; and debts were prolonged; transgressions were forgiven; the baptismal font was opened and many were baptized; the impure were made holy, and the earth rejoiced; Heaven exulted; the hosts of heaven sang, and shouted, saying, 'Glory be to God in the highest, and good will to all men; by the will of the Living God.' Luke ii. Thou therefore, my father, hast been praised and glorified 14 by men for a small and transitory work; and thou hast not thyself searched and wondered and confessed and glorified Him who in six days made all these things and created the creatures; nor our Lord Jesus the Christ, He who extended His grace upon the earth; and filled creation with His peace. And to the Living Spirit, who is the Holy Paraclete, who calleth all men to the kingdom of heaven."

And when the blessed Irene had said these things to her father, Licinius returned her an answer, saying, " I have had great patience with thy speech, my daughter, on account of thy sweet grace, because for years I have heard thy voice; and sweet to me is the sound of thy sentences. Therefore let us go into the city. And thou hast told me what thou desirest."

Then the king and his nobles led the blessed Irene and went into the city. But the queen her mother followed after her daughter bent in person, and she lifted the dust from beneath the feet of her daughter. And she applied it to her eyes and on her body, saying, "May this dust from beneath the holy feet of my beloved daughter be to me rest and healing, and for the redemption of my life and for the remission of sins, and for the new eternal life." And all the people who saw her, did likewise. And the king turned round, and saw [it], and commanded that no man should hinder them.

And when the blessed one had entered the city the magnates and the patricians and the patrician ladies came out to meet her, and they did obeisance to her, because they saw that she was lovely. But the plebeians and the poor people could not see her because of the great crush; for they were longing greatly to see her; and were running to the high places and standing, and studying her beauty from thence. And everyone who saw her was filled with great joy, as if they had already beheld the face of an angel. And when she came to enter by the door of her father's palace, a certain vicious demon met her, and said to her, "What is there between me and thee, thou hand-maid of Jesus? Get thee out of this city, for no Christian can dwell in it." But the blessed Irene said to that demon,

"Who art thou? and what is thy name?" The demon said, "Nargium is our name. And I guard this city, and many people are mine. I am the first charioteer of the gods; and I rejoice in quarrels, and exult in slaughter. And I excite disputes, and I rejoice in the shedding of blood. I supply the wizards, and enchain many by means of them. I am the father and the originator of all evils. I am the rock of adamant on which all the souls of the wicked shall be dashed. Now I have made known to thee my power and my courage. Therefore get thee away from the city, lest thou be angry, and I go to thy father, and ruin thee also."

Irene answered, "I say to thee, vile demon, and rabid imp, In the name of our Lord Jesus the Christ, it is not lawful for thee to be in this city, nor to ruin nor to hurt any one of its inhabitants. Therefore begone! lest I destroy thee in the name of Jesus."

But he, when he heard the glorious name of Jesus, fled in fear and trembling, and went out of the city astonished. And as he was going out, he approached the king and whispered in his ear, saying to him, "If thou art mine, Licinius, be strong and of good courage; for thy daughter is mixed up with the error of the Christians." And when he had said this, he went out of the city shaking and howling. And at the dawn of day the king called to the f. 114 a queen and said to her, "What shall we do, for our daughter is mixed up with the error of the Christians?"

The queen said, "Why dost thou think that our daughter is certainly in error? Be it far from her! let it not be! for our daughter has not erred and does not err."

The king said, "She confesses the Christ and denies the gods, does she not surely err?"

The queen said, "But the gods who did not make the heaven and the earth, how are they gods? I also say let them perish from beneath the sky. I disown them and those who worship them. Peace be to our daughter, and glory be to the Christ, who hath called her to immortal life."

Then the king was terribly angry, and he commanded that they should put the queen out of the palace; and that she should remain out of it. But one of the maidens ran and told Irene, "Thy father hath chased thy mother away because of thee." But when she heard it she said to the handmaiden, "Fear not, for beside me my father has the strength of an ant."

And the blessed one rose in haste, and went to the palace of her father, that she might enter his presence with all speed. But many of the magnates and of the king's servants prevented her and tried to persuade her not to do so[1], for they said to her, "Do not shew thyself to-day to thy father; because he is growling[2] like a lion to destroy thee." But when the blessed one heard it she laughed again and said : "As my Lord and my God Jesus liveth to-day and at this moment I will see him!"

f. 114 b

Now when they heard a knock at the king's door, they went in and made it known to the king, saying, "Thy daughter is standing without and desires to enter thy presence and see thee." When the king had heard it, he commanded her to enter. And the holy Irene entered and stood before her father. And when he saw her, he bent his head[3] down, and gazed on the ground in the anger of his mind. For he could not bear to look at her in the wrath of his heart. When Irene saw it, she said, "Why art thou of sad countenance to-day, my father, and not as usual. Thou hast one only daughter; and lo! she is standing before thee. Whereabouts in the palace is the queen, my mother and mistress dwelling? Is she well?"

But he did not answer her a word. Irene said, "Whence hath this anxiety [come] to thee, my father? And I do not know my own parent by reason of his sad countenance." And the king said, "Would that I had not begotten thee, my daughter! then I would not have fallen into this anxiety on thy account. I made a famous castle for thy sake; and I adorned it with all beautiful things; and I surrounded it with a strong wall; and I placed guards over it and I set up ninety-eight gods in it for thy glory and that they might protect thee. And I gave a table and a

---

[1] Literally "to enter his presence."
[2] Literally "gnashing."   [3] Literally "face."

candelabrum and a throne and all the vessels for thy service of wrought gold, and crowns of emeralds and gold, also pearls. I made thy dresses of all colours, of fine linen and of silk, and of spun gold, and all of them were beautiful. And hast thou repaid me for them, my daughter?" Irene said, "But what evil have I done to thee, my father?" The king said, "Is it a little thing to me, this anxiety and f. 115 a wrong which thou hast caused to me and hast repaid me [with]? Thou hast confessed the Christ, and hast believed in Jesus, and hast denied the gods."

Irene said, "That is not a wrong to thee, my father, that I have believed in the Christ. Nor again is it an anxiety to thee that I confess Jesus. I am hurting thee in nothing. For I rely on the Lord Jesus that thou also wilt soon confess and believe in the Christ. And I know not why thou art anxious."

The king said: "My beloved daughter Penelope, is it thy wish that I should not be anxious?" "Yes," said Irene. "Sacrifice to the gods," said the king.

Irene said, "My father, do not twist thy tongue, nor call me Penelope; do not change my name, for it is not Penelope."

"And what is thy name?" said the king to her.

Then she said: "Irene is my name, for by that name my betrothed and my God called me when I was in that castle which thou didst build for me."

But when the king heard it he was extremely angry, and said, "I renounce this child, artful for evil and not for good, and would that thou hadst never been!" Then the king commanded his magnates to take her away to the circus; and to bind her with ropes and throw her down and cause chariots with horses to run over her; that she might die by the trampling of horses and the wheels. And the servants of sin led her at once and bore her to the

circus. And with weeping and bitter tears they brought
her near the place in which there was to be an end to her
life. And after these things the king arose and went out
of the palace to go to the circus and see the death of his
daughter. And one of the noble horses who were there
who had been made chief of the stable, cut the ropes of his
halter and destroyed the stall in which he was standing and
ran straight on the king and bit him and he fell down and
died. And it seized his right arm and carried it away
from his shoulder, and he fell and died. And it returned
and stood in its stall where it had been standing. And
suddenly there was much mourning and weeping in the
king's house. But as for that horse to it was given the
speech of man, for the glory of God. And it spoke and
said thus : "Blessed art thou, Irene, handmaid of God, and
blessed art thou among women. Thou hast been delivered
into the hands of the wicked upon the earth, and in heaven
thine espousals and their adornment are prepared. Thou
hast wept upon earth, and in paradise thou shalt be embraced by the sweetness of heaven. Here thou art afflicted,
but thou shalt be made splendid beyond the splendour of
light. Thou art hated by many upon earth, but thou shalt
stand and be glorified beside Jesus thy betrothed. Blessed
be thou and blessed be thy soul."

Now when the horse had said these things, they led the
horses and brought them down to the circus. But that
horse remained apart from them ; because by reason of
its strength they were unable to bring it down with its
companions ; and because they were afraid that it might
kill them, like the king. Now it had happened to the
blessed Irene that they had bound her with ropes according
to the commandment of the king, and all the horses came
and knelt down and did obeisance before her. And all
the people were amazed at this wonder. And suddenly

her fetters were loosed from her; and they saw it and glorified God. And in that hour the servants of the king came and said to her, "A horse has bitten thy father and he is dead; and behold! he is thrown on the ground, and his arm is taken off."

And she said: "Fear not, he is not really dead, but is sleeping and this that has happened was for the glory of God. Ye also shall see [it,] and believe in God."

And when the great crowd heard that the king was dead, grief and sorrow overspread their mind; and they came and fell down before the feet of the blessed one, and did obeisance to her; and they persuaded her saying, "Lady, take pity on thy father who is dead; and it is grievous to thee, for his hand, too, has been taken away, and thrown aside."

And the blessed Irene came and stood over the corpse of her father. And all the people wondered; for they left off their mourning for the dead king, and were amazed at the speech of the horse and at the loosening of its bonds.

The holy Irene said: "Bring the hand that was cut off close to the place from which it was cut. And make it touch the place." And they did accordingly. Then Irene turned to the East, and lifted up her eyes[1] and her hands to heaven. And she prayed, with weeping and sobs, to God, saying, "God the Father in heaven, who hast established the foundations of the earth; Thou Rock that never movest, and fortress that never dost capitulate, Sun of Righteousness and path of life, and Way of salvation, who sittest on the right hand of Him who sent thee, O Lord, my God and my betrothed, Jesus the Christ, Son of the Living God, Thou who callest sinners to repentance, that they may turn to f. 116 b the knowledge of the truth and not perish, Merciful and Pitiful One, hearken to my voice, and look on the humble

_____
[1] Literally "glance."

estate of Thy handmaiden.   May Thy strong power come from heaven on this dead man and raise him up, that this crowd may see these things and believe and glorify Thy holy name ; and know that Thou art the Lord of the heaven and of the earth, and the Redeemer of all men who believe in Thee."

And when she had finished her prayer, the soul of that dead man entered into him, and he lived, and arose, and sat up.   And his daughter turned and saw him ; and she went up to him and took him with her hands and set him up, saying to him : " Rise, my father, by the power of Jesus." And he arose and walked to and fro, his hand that was cut off being quite whole, and not a blemish being on his body.

And when all the people saw it, they cried saying, " Great is the God of Irene and there is none but Him." And they believed, and turned to God : and three thousand people were baptized on that day.

Then Licinius the king took his daughter by the hand, blessing God and saying, " Great is the triumph of thy victory, my daughter ! and great thy promise in heaven. Thou art called the possession of Jesus, and the inheritance of the Christ ; O most fortunate of children ! O consolation and faith of parents !   Children like thee, my daughter, are able to save their fathers from a painful death !   Behold ! I also am henceforth a Christian, and a servant of Jesus. And henceforth I renounce this kingdom of the world that passeth away, and I look for the kingdom of heaven that passeth not away ; and I leave this kingdom to him who wishes to inherit it.   And I will take thy mother, my daughter, and I will go to the castle that I have built for thee ; and I also will see Jesus as thou hast seen Him ; and I will know Him like thee ; and I will be His own and will seek refuge in Him.   For I am unable to be king

f. 117 a

inasmuch as I have confessed Jesus and have been called a Christian; lest the neighbouring kings come upon me and destroy me from life. For I know and I believe that inasmuch as I have believed in Jesus, they will not be able to hurt me."

Then the king took the queen, and they went away to the castle, and were there confessing the Christ.

Then the blessed one remained in the city doing miracles, and signs of cures. And she taught the word of truth and instructed many; and baptized them in the name of the Father, and the Son, and the Holy Spirit.

After these things Zedekia the king heard what had become of king Licinius, and of the deeds which his daughter had done: and he was astonished. And he took a great and countless army, and went to Magdu, the city of king Licinius: and when he entered it and alighted in it, he called the magnates of the city, and asked them, "Where is your king?" And they returned him an answer and said, "He is dwelling in the castle which he had built for his daughter, he and his wife." The king said, "And his daughter, is she with him?" The f. 117 b magnates said, "No, my lord." The king said, "And where doth she dwell? Is she in the city?" They said, "She dwells with Apellianus her teacher."

And then the king sent to seek Apellianus the teacher. And he came, and stood in his presence. "Tell me," said the king, "thou old man, is the maiden, the daughter of king Licinius, with thee?" "Yes, my lord the king," said Apellianus. "What is her mind?" said the king, "and what are her meditations? dost thou not know?" "Her thoughts and her meditations," said Apellianus, "are mine and those of all who fear God. For from evening till evening she partakes of an ounce of bread, and drinks a sixth part of a hemina of water. She knows not a table,

L. E.

P

nor is she acquainted with a bed, and neither by night nor by day does she cease from the praise of God, and her eye is never done with tears."

And when the king heard it, he was greatly astonished. And at the dawn of day he sent Euphorba with ten chief men to king Licinius, to that castle, and they said to him, "O king, live for ever! Come to our city and receive us, as is thy good custom. What is this that thou hast done? Art thou making a trial of us? Come to thine own palace."

But when the magnates had said these things to Licinius the king, he said to them, "Go ye and say to the king who sent you, 'O noble king, live for ever! My kingdom is given unto thee.'"

Now when king Zedekia heard these things, he went into the palace of king Licinius; and he took his kingdom and inherited everything that he possessed.

f. 118 a

And on the following day king Zedekia sent his secretary and his great men for the maiden Irene, because of the honour [due to] her father. And the Hyparch and the magnates who were with him went to the house of Apellianus, to Irene; and they said to her, "O daughter of a king! behold the king seeks thee."

And she arose with great joy, and went, and entered the king's presence, and stood before him. And when the king saw her, he said, "Peace be to thee!" But she did not answer him a word. And after a little while she said to him, "Why didst thou call for me?" The king said, "Let us sit and talk about the peace of the city."

Ps. i. 1

Irene said, "I will not sit with iniquitous people, nor will I enter into the assembly of the sinners; nor will I sit upon the seat of the scorners." "Am I then a sinner and an iniquitous man?" said the king. Irene said, "Truly every one who is a pagan is wicked and iniquitous."

But when the king heard [it] he was exceedingly wroth, and was filled with threatenings: and he said, "Irene, sacrifice to the gods!" Irene said, "In vain art thou disturbed, O king! Satan, thy father, excites thee and inflames thee against me. But I do not fear thy threats; because I have believed in Jesus. And He saves me from all thy wiles, and all thy hateful counsels concerning me are useless." And the king commanded them to dig a pit thirty cubits wide and thirty cubits deep, and to throw wild beasts into it, and snakes, and scorpions, and asps, and serpents, and vipers, and all the stinging things of Satan. And the servants of wickedness did accordingly.

And the king commanded them to bring the blessed f. 118 b Irene, and to carry her and throw her into that pit. And the servants of sin led her and carried her thither. And they said to her, weeping, "Why dost thou not sacrifice, O daughter of the king, and live? but thou hast made this choice for thyself to die a grievous death." But she said, "Be silent, for ye know not what ye are saying."

And that blessed one looked down into the pit and saw all the reptiles that were in it, and she said, "How shall I go down?" And they said, "The king has commanded that thou shalt be thrown head downwards into it."

Then Irene lifted up her hands and raised her eyes[1] upwards, weeping; and she prayed to Jesus, saying, "O Lord the Christ, behold, for Thy sake I bear these things. And I go down into this pit [leaning] on the power of Thy divinity. Show Thy favour to me, O Lord, and let the iniquitous people and their father, Satan, be ashamed."

And she made the sign of Jesus between her eyes, and on her breasts, and threw herself head downwards into the midst of the pit. And when she reached the bottom, all these reptiles ran away from before her, and stuck to the

[1] Literally, "glance."

walls of the pit; and had stuck [to them] and died.   And the blessed Irene opened her mouth and prayed, saying, "I confess to thee, O Lord, whose are the heaven and the earth, that Thou art from everlasting to everlasting.   Thou hast created all men, O Lord, upon the earth.   Thou didst send our Lord Jesus the Christ, Thy Son, and Thy Beloved, for the redemption of the world; and He came and was born of Mary the Virgin; and He conquered all the power of the enmity of Satan; and frustrated all his wiles; and He gave strength and power to those men who worship Him and believe in Him, that they should tread on the wild beasts, and the scorpions, and the serpents, and the vipers, and on all the stinging things of the enmity of Satan.   And Thou hast to-day shown Thy grace towards the weakness of Thy handmaiden.   And Thou hast slain all these evil reptiles by Thy strong power and Thy swift commandment.   And Thou hast saved me by the help of Thy favour.   I confess to Thee and I give Thee glory that Thou hast not overlooked my low estate.   And Thy grace has come to my help.   And Thou hast kept me as the apple of the eye."

And she was in the pit for fourteen days, and she took no nourishment.   But she was fed by the Holy Spirit. And it was told to the king that all these evil reptiles had died; and had stuck to the walls in dying.   And the king and his magnates were greatly astonished when they heard it.   And on the following day the king called her and said to her, "Irene, sacrifice to the gods!   Behold, thou hast killed all the reptiles, and thou art alive."

Irene said, "O many headed Satan! is this thy question with me?   But I ask thee, O son of deceit, tell me." She said, "Has the weak power of thy gods done any enchantments like these? or is there any power like this that they have killed evil reptiles? except the power of Jesus?"

f. 119 a

But when the king heard this, he was filled with f. 119 b
rage and said, "Bring me hither two carpenters and two
saws." And they brought [them] to him as he had said.
And he commanded them to squeeze the lamb of the
Christ in the press of the carpenters, and to saw her in
twain. And the servants of sin did according to the
commandment of the king; and they squeezed her in
the press. And they placed a saw above her head; and
the carpenters lifted them up to saw her; and the saw
became blunted, and did not hurt the body of the maiden.
When the judge saw that the saw did not touch her
body, he commanded that there should be a tall engine,
and that they should tie her there to stakes, and saw
her in twain. And the engine came; and they tied the
blessed one to it, and they placed the saw above her
head. And they let go the saw, and in that hour the
saw was cleft in twain; and the carpenters fell from the
engine; and they also were cleft and died. And the
king saw that the two carpenters were dead, and that
the saw was cleft. And he turned towards all the people
and said, "They have made the engine idiotically, and they
have let the saw go suddenly, and it was cleft, and the
engine is fallen, and they are dead. It has befallen them
well; for it was not right for them to meddle with a matter
that was too difficult for them, and that they knew nothing
about, I am free from their mistake and from their blood."
And he commanded that there should be a saw double the
size of the one which was cleft. And they squeezed the
blessed one again into the carpenter's press; and began
again to saw her. And that saw was melted like wax.

And the believing woman laughed at their tortures and f. 120 a
[their] sawing; and her body was not hurt, and her colour
was not changed: and she gave glory to God.

And when the king saw that it profited nothing, he
commanded them to bring a great saw, and to bring a huge

stone of five hundred pounds [weight] and they put it on her breast; and that they should saw her feet off from her knees. And the servants of sin did accordingly; and they sawed off the feet of the blessed one.

But she was singing praises to God with joy and with a loud voice. And she did not feel the pain. And when the king saw that the feet of the blessed one were cut off, he laughed, and said, "Irene, where is thy God? let Him come now and deliver thee from my hands, if He can." Irene said, "By the life of Jesus who has redeemed me and is redeeming me, for there is no grace for thee."

And the king was enraged and blasphemed God; for the bystanders were afraid to weep openly in his presence but they wept in secret and murmured, saying, "Bitter are the punishments of the king and iniquitous are his commandments." For they took pity on the beauty of the maiden and on her youth.

And suddenly the air was aflame, and there were fearful thunderings and fierce lightnings; and terrible noises and mighty voices, like none that had ever been before. And darkness overspread the earth, and the earth trembled; and a voice of the trumpeting of angels came from the sky[1]. And when the king saw it, he feared greatly, and said, "Let us flee to the city! let every man flee to his house!" And the king fled and those who were with him to get into the city. And the blessed one remained with her feet cut off, and that stone lying on her breasts. The king said, "Lift it away. Now we will see if the Christ will come to deliver her." And when they had lifted it, and all the people had fled, one of the harlots remained beside her whose name was Curica. She said to the blessed one, "I will not leave thee, thou handmaid of the Christ! with thee I will die, and with thee I will live in life eternal."

f. 120 b

---

[1] Literally "air."

But as for the king and the great men who were with
him who had fled, that they might go into the city, they
imagined that he had gone before them ; justice was behind
them bringing (him) to them.   And they had come un-
willingly, and stood beside the blessed one, and then they
knew that God had come near on her behalf.   And when
the king saw that harlot beside her, he commanded, and
they beheaded her with the sword.   And when she was
dying the handmaid of the Christ said, "Pray for me,
that I may not be separated from thee."   And Irene
sealed her in the name of the Father, and the Son, and
the Holy Spirit.   And she stretched out her neck and
received joyfully the crown of martyrdom by the sword.
And suddenly God cast fear upon the king and upon his
great men, and they arose affrighted and were silent in
astonishment ; and were unable to walk hither or thither.
Then two angels came down from heaven by the com-   f. 121 a
mandment of God, beside the virgin of the Christ, and they
loosed her from her bonds, and rolled away the stone
from her breasts ; and took up her feet which had been
cut off, and brought them close to the places from which
they had been severed.   And the blessed one was healed
and arose sound in body.   And they went up to heaven.

And the handmaiden of the Christ sang praises to God
without ceasing.   And she ran and reached the city before
the king.   But a current of air followed the king and his
magnates, it was very cold by reason of the hail which
had come ; and it slew three thousand men of these pagans,
but it did not hurt the king ; because he was kept for the
wrath to come.

And the people who were left cried out, saying, " Truly
great is the God of Irene, and there is none but He."   And
they called on the Lord, saying, " Have mercy upon us,
O God ! according to Thy grace, and blot out our sins in

Thy compassion. Forgive us our iniquity in Thy pity, because our hope is in Thee; and in Thee we take refuge." And on that day eight thousand souls believed.

And the king called the damsel, and said to her, "Lo! thou hast killed three thousand people with thine enchantments, and thou hast snatched away eight thousand from the gods. When they saw that thy feet were healed they believed in thy God. Now approach and sacrifice, lest thy life vanish miserably from the world."

Irene said, "O furnace of falsehood......of error, son of Satan! art thou not ashamed and dost thou not fear God? Thou hast not laid to heart the coldness of the air which f. 121 b occurred. And did not trembling dwell in thy heart at the death of thy wicked comrades? and didst thou not fear Him who saved thee from a death like theirs[1]? For thou didst not escape from that death because of thy righteousness, but that the crown of my martyrdom might be plaited and adorned by thy hands."

And when the king had heard (this) he was filled with a great rage, and he called the Eparch, and said to him, "Wilt thou not say by what kind of death I shall slay that [woman] of hateful name?" The Eparch said, "Let them carry her to where there is a mill; and let them bind her against the spoke of the wheel; and let them fix iron hooks on the ends of the spokes, and let the water on to the wheel. And when the force of the water shall strike on the wheel and it shall revolve, the hooks will take away from her sides, and thus the disappearance of her life from the world will be very grievous." And the servants of sin did thus, and they fixed wood against the wheel, and bound the virgin of the Christ to it. And they let out the water at the wheel, and at once the water became hard as stone, and did not move. And the wheel did not tremble, and

---

[1] Literally "from their death."

the body of the blessed one was unhurt. But the king and the magnates who were standing round him were amazed. And the blessed Irene laughed and said to them, mocking, "O mistaken people! Ye have made instruments of torture after your own pleasure by your commandment, and they do not obey you. And in vain do ye weary yourselves...... therefore do what is incumbent on you......that...of fortitude, and my heroism may be made known to you and to many." But the king and his magnates said to her, "Irene, why dost thou not sacrifice to the gods?" And she said, "Because of the hour of the trumpet which will bring you to life." f. 122 a

Then she said, "When I have truly seen dogs encompassing me, and the assembly of the wicked have enclosed me, as David has said, 'The wicked walk on every side, like the vile exaltation of the sons of Edom, and their words are softer than oil, yet are they javelins; their tongue is as a sharp sword; and their poison is like that of cruel vipers. They have compassed me like hornets, they are quenched as the fire of stubble. Their sword shall enter into their heart, and their bows shall be broken.' O hypocrites! hearken and understand, that the prophecy has said these things against you." Ps. xxii. 16 Ps. xii. 8 Ps. lv. 21 Ps. cxviii. 12 Ps. xxxvii. 15

The king said, "Irene, come, go up the ascent of the mill-wheel, till my mind takes counsel and my intelligence devises[1] tortures that are more bitter than these for thee." And when she had gone up, he commanded that she should be bound in the prison-house. And the servants of sin carried her and shut her up in the prison-house. And suddenly God cast contentions into the minds of all the citizens, and excited them against the king. And they raised a persecution against him, and the patricians and the plebeians of the whole city were assembled, and they

---

[1] Literally "begets."

said to him, "As for thee, what art thou doing in our city?
and why dost thou sit in a palace which is not thine own?
Get thee out of our city, for thou art not our king. Long
live our king Licinius!" Then they stoned him and put
him out of their city, and he went to his city. And in
f. 122 b seven days he died, and Severon his son reigned after him.
And twenty days after the death of his father, he assembled
a great army, about a hundred thousand fighting men.
And he purposed in his mind that he would go to the city
of Magdo, and lay it waste, and avenge by its means the
insult [done] to his father, and his death. For he went to
that city filled with anger and rage, and he threatened
concerning it that he would swallow it like a dragon. For
when those citizens had heard [of it] fear fell upon them,
and they said to Irene, "My lady, perhaps it is for thy
sake that our city is desolate and we are dying"; and they
closed the gates of the city, and none might go out and
none might enter for fear of the king; for there were a
hundred thousand fighting men with him, besides many
others who were allied with him, for they came because
of the spoiling of the city. And when the blessed one
saw that the citizens were disturbed and were weeping,
she said to them, "Peace be to you. Fear not. I will go
out and go on to meet him."

But they said to her, "We implore of thee, lady, we
shall die and our city will be laid waste; but thou shalt
not go out to any place; and thou shalt not go near him,
lest he slay thee."

But a certain faithful man was there, whose name was
Alexander. He said to the citizens, "You are making a
f. 123 a mistake by too great haste. This is she who has slain all
that bad vermin by the power of God; and she has also
raised up her father, and she has brought down an angel
from above by her prayer; and she has done many signs.

Does she fear the rustle of the wing of this locust? For are not his threats weak beside the strength of this valiant woman? Fear not therefore." But when they heard these words, they opened the gates of the city and allowed her to go out.

And she went and reached the king's presence. And she saw his numerous troops surrounding him. And she turned to the east and raised her hands and her eyes[1] aloft. And she prayed and said, "O Lord God! whose are the heaven and the earth, as Thou didst hear the voice of Elisha the prophet, and didst strike the people with a phantom, show the wonder here also, and hearken to the voice of the prayer of Thy handmaid and show the power of Thy might this day, and strike this people with a phantom, and keep the light of day from their eyes, because they are going to lay waste an innocent city; and they threaten to destroy the life of many persons." And when she had finished her prayer, the Lord smote that people with a phantom. And as for the king, his limbs were loosened, and his chiefs beheld that their light[2] was taken from them. He said to Irene, "Irene, now I know that the power of God accompanies thee. Pray for us to thy God, and we shall see the light." II Kings vi. 18 f. 123 b

And she bent the knee and prayed to God, and their eyes were opened, and they saw the light. And their limbs also which had been loosened, were healed. And the king and his great men entered the city, and the great army that was with him; and the blessed Irene. And in the morning he assembled the whole city and said to them persuasively, "Peace be unto you. Fear not, there will be no trouble to any man in your city. There is quiet and peace between me and you."

[1] Or "glance."

[2] The MS. adds, "And the king's limbs were loosened along with his being bereft of light."

And the next day the king said, "Call Irene to me."
And they called her and brought her. And they said,
"Lo! she is standing before thy majesty." The king said,
"Irene, I have forgiven the fault of the city, but I will not
forgive thee, because thou wert the hateful cause of the
stoning of my father; and he was stoned, and he died.
Now if thou desirest that I should not requite at thy hands
the contumely and the blood of my father, sacrifice to the
gods."

Irene said, "Thou art cursed by God [thou] and thy
counsel. But do not thou trifle, but turn to the counsel
of thy father, Satan. And what he advises, do it to me
quickly and without delay, that thou also mayest know
the power of God that is in me."

And the king was wroth with a very great wrath. And
he commanded concerning her that she should be kept in
the prison-house. And they carried her to the prison-
house. And the king said to his great men, "With what
torture ought we to kill her?" And they said to him what
Satan had sown in their hearts, "Let thy majesty command
them to bring three hundred of the best nails, and let
them be fixed under her feet. And let sand be dropped
into a sack and let her carry it on her shoulders. And let
them put a muzzle in her mouth and let one of the soldiers
lead her and conduct her for five miles, and make her
return [for] five. With this torture she will sacrifice or die."

f. 124 a   And whilst she was in the prison, our Lord Jesus the
Christ appeared to her, and a host of angels. And He
said to her, "Irene, fear not, for I am with thee; and my
Father, with the Holy Spirit, are helping with thy struggle.
And all the armies of heaven are helping with thy conflict.
And even the bones of the righteous fathers delight in
thy victory." And our Lord set His seal upon her, and
ascended up to heaven with His holy angels.

And Irene was in the prison-house for fourteen days. And at the end of fourteen days the king called her and said to her, "Irene, sacrifice to the gods. Hearken to my voice, that thou die not very badly."

But she answered him not a word. And when the king saw that she gave him no answer, he was filled with a great anger. And the king commanded, [saying,] "Bring me three hundred nails, and fasten them under her feet, and load her with a sack of sand, and thrust a muzzle in her mouth; and let a soldier lead her like a beast." And the servants of sin made her run five miles, and made her return five miles. But the blessed lamb of the Christ did not feel the pain in her feet, and the suffering did not reach her heart. And when they brought her into the city, many of the pagans were laughing at her and saying, "Where is Jesus? Is He not coming to save her now?"

But the blessed one saw an angel who was standing before her. And he held a rod of iron and struck it on the earth saying thus: "The engulfing of the enemies of righteousness to-day." And when the blessed one came and arrived at the place where she had seen the angel standing, the earth opened its mouth and swallowed up the f. 124 b servants of sin, and many pagans. And the nails were taken away from her feet, and the sack of sand that she carried; and the muzzle was taken from her mouth, and they were swallowed up with the infidels. And when the king saw this sign of a wonder, he was amazed and astonished. And he turned round and said to the crowd of the infidels, "They had sinned some sin before the gods, therefore hath the earth swallowed them up." And in all these things the heart of the king was hardened, and that of his magnates, and they believed not in God. And the angel of God turned hastily towards the assembly of the wicked, and he slew many of them. But the number of those who were engulfed with those who died was ten thousand ; and those who were left cried to the Lord God, saying, " Have mercy upon us. oh God! and forgive us our sins by Thy grace, and be reconciled to us, according to Thy mercies ; for Thou art the merciful God, who hast done many wonders by the hand of Irene." And three thousand souls believed in God at that moment.

And as the king did not wish to believe, the Lord smote him and slew him.

But the blessed lamb of the Christ went into the city, and taught many, and baptized them in the name of the Father, and the Son, and the Holy Spirit. And they brought near to her those who were sick with various and hateful diseases, and she cured them by the power of God. For the grace of God accompanied the holy Irene. And moreover they brought near to her those in whom there were evil spirits, and she cured them by the power of God. And she chased away the demons. And they brought to her a certain six years old boy, in whom was an evil spirit, which withered him up.

f. 125 a

And when she saw it she was grieved on account of his youth. And she asked the mother of the boy : " How old is this child ? " And the boy's mother said : " Six years old, lady." And the blessed one, the handmaid of the Christ, took pity on the boy. And she lifted him up in her arms, and sealed him in the name of the Father, and the Son, and the Holy Ghost. And she prayed and said : " God who has created man in His image, the merciful, the pitiful, He who has said : ' I do not wish the death or destruction of men,' O Lord God! whose are the heaven and the earth, rebuke Satan and all his temptations, and look on the tender age of this boy, and send him help from Thy sanctuary, and let all men know that Thou hast answered them who call upon Thee in truth ; and shew the sign of Thy miracle in him who has wronged this boy, and may this demon speak and make [himself] known to me."

And when the blessed one had prayed and finished her prayer, the angel of God bound the demon and set him before her. And when she saw the demon, she said to him, "Tell me, thou unclean demon, why hast thou subjugated this boy and spoilt his youth?" Said the demon: "I implore thee, my lady, I have surely been sent." Irene said: "God doth not tempt, and willeth not the death of man. Tell me, therefore, who hath sent thee." The demon answered: "Wicked men who treat each other badly." Irene said: "Shew me who it is that sent thee." f. 125 b Said the demon: "I have told thee, my lady, that they are wizards, the enemies of the justice of God, and our friends. Therefore we are sent by them for vengeance. And we go wheresoever we are sent. And some men we corrupt, and some we paralyse; and some of them we put to death in ways that are bad and varied."

Irene said: "Bring them to me, those who have sent thee." The demon said: "My lady, whilst I am standing here I will tell thee their names."

Irene said: "Who are they?" The demon said: "I implore of thee, my lady, Amos and Euteles, they who have a bazaar near the great portico of the Temple of Fortune of the city, and who have also a bank."

Then she sent and had them both brought, and she said to them, "Hear ye what this demon saith? Look if he be speaking the truth. And I will not loose the demon; because a demon has never spoken the truth, and see if ye have sent him; and so far as I think, he speaks the truth from fear, for no demon is able to stand up before the servants of God and lie, for he fears lest they should destroy him."

And the holy Irene turned towards all the people, and said: "Brethren, do not believe the demon, because he is a liar, and does not desire the quiet of men, but wars and contentions; because he is the enemy of justice. But I ask you to tell me the truth. Has it ever been heard by you about these men that they are malefactors?"

They said, "Yes, lady, they are bad, and their parents also followed these bad courses, and they have corrupted and destroyed many people of the city."

f. 126 a

And she said to these two bad men, "Verily ye have sinned like men and have made God angry, but now repent towards Him; and your sins shall be forgiven; and your debts shall be blotted out."

And they returned her an answer: "But as for us, lady, we do not know what thou hast said, and we cannot approach to that business." And when Irene saw that they denied about their deeds and that they did not want to confess and repent towards God, she said to them: "Ye yourselves know; I am freed from your blood." And she looked to heaven and said: "Lord Jesus the Christ, Son of the Living God, if it be true what they say about these men, and if they do not want to confess and repent, shew concerning them a sign of miracle in the sight of every one; and let those who are standing here see and know that Thou only art the God of truth." And immediately a fire was kindled in their hearts, and it took hold of their bodies, and they were burnt. For the burning came from themselves and amongst them, and they were like a flaming furnace. And they burned and became like burnt firebrands. And when they saw them a great fear fell amongst them. And after these things she lifted the boy in her arms, and looked to heaven and prayed. And she sealed him in the name of the Father, and Son, and Holy Spirit. And he was healed and she gave him quite whole to his mother.

But when the great crowd who were standing there saw the death and destruction of the wicked people, and the healing of the boy, they gave praise to God and shouted, saying, "Great is the God of Irene."

And after two days some people were carrying a certain f. 126 b young man and were going out to bury him. And the blessed Irene saw that his parents were weeping, and were lamenting bitterly over him, because he was their only son. And she was grieved. And the father of the young man who had died, when he saw the holy Irene, came and fell on his face before her feet, saying to her, while prostrate, " I beseech thee, lady, have pity on the humiliation of my grey hairs. This was the only son I had. And if thou wilt, pray to God that he may live. For we also are Christians, lady, and disciples of the Word of thy holiness, and by means of thee we have known the Living God."

And she took pity on his old age, and went with him to those who were carrying the bier. And she spake to the bearers and they laid the bier down on the earth. And she turned to the whole crowd and said, " My fellow believers, offer prayer to God with me." And she stretched out her hands and looked[1] towards heaven, and prayed, saying, " O Lord God, King of the ages, He who sitteth on the cherubim and the seraphim stand before Him : and the angels and the archangels and all the hosts of heaven serve Him with fear. O God who didst shew wonders by the hands of the prophets and of the holy fathers ; Lord of the righteous, and Lover of the penitent; He whom the prophets sought for and whose faith the Apostles preached : in the created [world] by Jesus the Christ, the Son of the Living God ; He who said, ' He that believeth John xiv. on me, greater works than these which I do, shall he 12

---

[1] Literally, "and her look."

do.' He who gave life to the only son of the widow, and snatched the daughter of Jairus from death by His hand.

f. 127 a He who called Lazarus out of the grave, and brought him up out of Sheol, the voracious pit. And now, Lord, Thou art and Thou dost exist for ever. Shew, Lord, the power of Thy might in this dead man, and let him live, and stand up; because he also is the only son of his parents. And let these multitudes see [it] and praise Thy holy name. And let all the erring ones turn towards Thee."

And when she had finished her prayer, the dead man lived and arose and ran and came before her and adored her. But when these crowds saw it they were astonished and they praised God. And many believed in God on that day. And on that day, by the will of God, Timothy the holy priest came to the holy woman. And she saw him and rejoiced with great joy. And she ran and did obeisance to him as to the apostle of Jesus. And she led him and went to the castle where her father and her mother dwelt. And she said to the great crowd of the believers, " My brethren, be active, and come with me as far as the castle." And as they were on their way, it was told to Licinius her father, " Thy daughter and a priest of God are coming towards thee." And when he heard [it], he rejoiced with great joy. And when he saw the great crowd that was coming, he commanded that all the gates of the wall should be opened, and the gates of the castle itself. And the king and queen ran and went joyfully out to meet the holy priest, and Irene their daughter. For their mind exulted·when they heard that their daughter was alive, and was coming towards them.

f. 127 b And when they saw their daughter with the holy priest, they ran and did obeisance to him[1]. And they wept and

---

[1] Literally, "to the holy priest."

kissed and embraced their daughter lovingly, and praised
God. For they had imagined that their daughter was dead.
And when they saw her in life, they rejoiced and praised
God. And the blessed one turned to her father and her
mother, and said to them, "Peace be to you, my beloved
parents. Be not troubled and weep not, for behold God hath
given you His grace, and by means of the fruit of your
blood ye have known God." And she turned to the holy
priest and said to him, "I beseech of thee, my lord, priest
of the living God, complete thy blessing and thy favour to
my weakness; and baptize my father and my mother,
and the many young men who are hoping to receive the
symbol of the Christ": and she said to her father and
to her mother, "Dear parents, behold [, this is] the day
when your debts shall be wiped out, and ye shall be
washed from the filth of your sins. Behold, our Lord
Jesus hath sent the holy priest. Take the baptism and
receive the symbol of the Christ; and partake of the
marriage feast of the heavenly king." And they said,
"And what may prevent it, O beloved daughter?"

And the priest took the oil, and blessed and anointed
them, and he blessed upon and sanctified the water, and
baptized the king and the queen and also the soldiers:
and [of] the troops of the king four hundred persons who
were with them, and fifty thousand persons of the many
people who had come there. And after the holy priest had
baptized them, the holy Irene greeted[1] her father and her f. 128 a
mother, and all the rest of the household. And the blessed
one commanded them and said to them, "Be confirmed
in what ye have received. Be valiant in Jesus, and be
strong in the faith. Lo! ye have received baptism. Your
bodies are cleansed, and ye are mingled with the sheep
of Jesus. Your hearts are sanctified to be a dwelling-

---

[1] Literally, "gave peace to."

place of Jesus." And she said to them, "Abide in peace, and if it please the Lord Jesus, I will see you again." And she went out of the castle with the priest, and many people. But the king and the queen remained in the castle, and the four hundred persons who were with them, who had been baptized, praising God, and there was great joy in that city.

And afterwards two lepers drew near to her, who came from a far country. And she saw the dust that was upon their faces, and that their shoes were split, and she knew that they had come from afar. And she said to them, "Why have ye come to me? Behold, I am a weak woman, commonplace and feeble, and I possess nothing in this world, and I am a sinner." But they said to her, "O lady! thou doest well to humble thyself in [relation to] thine own will. But towards God thou art elect and great. And thou dost fulfil the word of Jesus thy Bridegroom; for thou hast heard that He said, 'Whosoever humbleth himself shall be exalted.'"

Luke xviii. 14

And those people threw themselves down on the ground before her feet, and they wept and said, "If thou wilt, lady, pray for us to God, and we shall be cleansed from our leprosy."

Then the holy one threw herself down before the Lord and shed tears with sobs, and prayed, saying, "O Lord God, to whom belongs the heaven and the earth, hearken unto the voice of Thy handmaid. And in Thy compassion grant my request: and may Thy power come from on high on the bodies of these people, and may they be cleansed, and let many see [it] and praise Thy great and fearful name." And whilst she was praying, the angel of God came and stood before her. And he said to her, "Peace be unto thee, Irene, virgin of the Christ."

f. 128 b

And when she saw the angel, she said, "Blessed be

Thou, O God, to whom belongs the heaven and the earth, for Thou hast heard the voice of Thy humble servant, and hast not turned away Thy face from me. But Thou hast sent Thine angel from on high from before Thy holy throne; and he has come to heal and to cleanse the bodies of these people." And immediately a fountain of water sprang up there. And when the blessed one saw it[1], she praised God and said, "This spring is from the holy water of Jordan, of that which Elisha the prophet blessed; and the Lord of Elisha blessed [it] by His baptism."

And she said to these men, "Go in and wash in that water, confessing the Father, and the Son, and the Holy Spirit; and your bodies shall be cleansed, and shall become tender as infants." Then these men went with great fear into the fountain of water, saying, "We confess the name of the Father, and the Son, and the Holy Ghost." And they came out of the fountain with their bodies cleansed, and fear and astonishment took hold of the great crowd f. 129 a that was there, and they praised God that the blessed Irene, the virgin of the Christ, had done these miracles and cures.

And she was three years in that city. And when Zedekiah and Severon his son were dead, Numerianus reigned after them, the son of Septinus. And he inquired about the blessed Irene. And he said, "Where is she?" And they said to him, "She is here in the city." And he sent soldiers, and commanded them, and said that they should "bring her to the city of Callinicus; and let her be kept there until I come." And the soldiers found her, those who went out after her; and they brought her to the city of Callinicus; and there she was carefully kept in the prison-house until the king should come there. And when he came, they informed him [saying], "Irene is there, she

---

[1] Literally, "the fountain of water."

whom thy Majesty asked for." And he commanded, "Bring her to me." And she came and stood before him. And when the king saw her, he was astonished.

And he said to his great men, "Hallo! this maiden is very like her father." And he said, "This girl is [the daughter] of Licinius; he forsook his kingdom, and renounced it; and now this city is without a king. On her account Zedekiah my brother was stoned and died. And because of her the angel of the Lord smote Severon his son and slew him. And I seek to requite their blood at her hands. And I fear lest a fate worse than that of my colleagues should befall me. Truly, as I see, this woman is a destroyer of the kingdom and also an overturner of kings. And I know not what I shall do to her." And he turned and said to the advocates who were standing in his presence, "Advise me in your wisdom by what torment I shall destroy her from the world. She has killed my father[1], and Zedekiah my brother; and she caused Severon his son to perish from the world. And what will she do to me? She is the extirpator of royalty." The magnates said to him, "Truly thou hast spoken well, O lord the king." Then the king commanded that they should bring her before him, and they brought her, and she stood before him.

f. 129 b

The king said, "Irene, what dost thou say? Wilt thou sacrifice to the gods or wilt thou be obstinate? and dost thou persist in the folly of the Christians?"

Irene said, "Because thou hast repeatedly said that I am the overturner of royalty, I say to thee, that thou also, if thou dost not believe in God, in a very little while the judgment of God shall overtake thee also; and thou shalt die a frightful and uncommon death. And then thou shalt know that there is a God who rules in the heaven

---

[1] Cod. "her father."

and in the earth." And when the king had heard [it] he was filled with great rage; and he commanded, "Bring me men who are artificers in copper." And they came and stood before him. The king said to them, "Make me three very large cows." And they made them and brought them to him. And he commanded that they should be greatly heated. And these cows were heated for three days and three nights, until the copper was nearly melted. And when the cows were heated, he commanded, and they brought Irene before him. The king said, "Irene, what sayest thou? I have commanded that there should be f. 130 a three cows of copper on thy account. And [here] they are. And I have commanded that they should be heated. And they are also heated frightfully. Now if thou wilt sacrifice to the gods, thou shalt be delivered from a frightful and terrible death. But if thou wilt not sacrifice, thou shalt be cast into the cows and shalt be burnt, and shalt die a very hard death. And if thou shouldst conquer the one by thy witchcraft, thou shalt be cast into the other; and if again thou shouldst conquer the second one by thy skill, thou shalt be cast into the third, and shalt perish. And very grievously shalt thou depart. And we shall see if Jesus will come, He in whom thou believest, and will save thee from my hands. Approach, therefore, and sacrifice to the gods."

Irene said, "Be not troubled, O son of Satan; for however much thy father Satan hath excited thee against me, I am not afraid of thee, neither now do thy threats move me. See therefore that thou explain to me in the skill of thy deceitful teaching, the stripes and the torments of thy contrivances." Then the king was greatly enraged, and said to her, "Cursed child! slayer of its parents, extirpator of royalty, thou hast called me senseless, I will shew thee what sense there is in me, by means of the torments that

my mind shall devise against thee." And he commanded
them to carry her out, and to heat these copper cows.
And he commanded the heralds to go out into the city
and proclaim that all men should come and see the
punishment and procession of the infidel despiser of the
gods. And when all the city was assembled, the king
came and sat on his judgment-seat, and he commanded
them: "Bring before me the audacious one, the parricide."
And she came and stood before him. The king said, "Irene,
f. 130 b choose between two things, either sacrifice to the gods, or
go into the copper cow."

Irene said, "O senseless fool, and ignorant sinner! son
of Satan the coiling serpent! I have said to thee once
[for all] that I am a Christian ; and I will not sacrifice to
the infidel demons nor to the foul fiends ; and I will not
forsake Jesus the Christ, my Lord ; and I shall not be
forsaken by Him. And these cows which flame by means
of thine evil skill, are to me fountains of cold water by the
help of Jesus, and they are of no account to me. For thou
shalt see quickly the power of the Lord Jesus to help that
is with me. And as for thee, His wrath is ready to come
upon thee by means of a terrible angel. And thou shalt
die a fearful and uncommon death ; not like thy predecessors, but thou shalt die the fearful death of terror.
And thine [own] liver shall be thy food, and thy lung thy
sustenance. And thy punishment shall be from thyself
and in thyself. And thou shalt know that there is a God
in heaven." Then the king waxed exceeding wroth, and
was like a lion eager to rend. And he commanded them
to throw her into the copper cow. And when she heard
[it,] before the servants of sin had laid hold of her and led
her out, she made the sign of Jesus on her breasts and
between her eyes, and she ran boldly to the copper cow
and went in. And immediately the fire was quenched ;

and the handmaid of the Christ was set free like a ship on a peaceful sea; and waters flowed from the cow itself. But when the judge saw it, he said to the people, "Did I not tell you that she would conquer by her witchcraft?"

But all the people wept bitterly, when they saw the f. 131 a beauty of her youth, and what torments she suffered.

Then she prayed in God's presence and said, "O Lord God, who dwellest in the highest heavens! hearken to my voice, and let Thy mercy come hither. See, because of Thy name I suffer these things. This I know, that Thou hast helped me and wilt help me. But because of these crowds, that they may see the sign of a miracle and may praise Thy name." And when she had said these things and had prayed, she saw the angel of God standing beside her. And he said to her, "Peace be to thee, Irene; fear not, for the Lord is with thee, and I have been sent for thy comfort." And she rejoiced and exulted at the sight of the angel.

And then the king commanded them to throw her into the second cow. Irene said, "O Satan, and son of Satan, and enemy of justice, if thou hast not been confounded by the first cow, thou shalt be confounded by this second one; and thou shalt despise thyself. And if again thou art not moved by the second, thou shalt be confounded by the end of the third, and shalt blush, when the wrath of the Lord shall come suddenly upon thee."

And he commanded them to throw her into the second cow. But when she heard it, she sealed herself in the name of the Father, and the Son, and the Holy Ghost. And she went into the cow rejoicing and exulting in the power of Jesus to help. And immediately the fire was quenched, and the flame was cooled, and the cow was melted like wax; and the blessed one was not hurt. And when the king again saw [it] he said to his magnates,

"Did I not tell you that she would conquer the fire by her witchcraft?"

f. 131 b   And the king commanded them to throw her into the third cow. But when she had heard it, she blessed God and said to the judge, "Thy torments are very insipid and thy fire is very cool. Thou art a serpent with many heads, and with thee are thy servants. For as for these cows, water instead of fire has come to them." And she went joyfully into the third cow in the strength of Jesus, laughing at them, for the pagans imagined that there her destruction would be. But when the blessed one entered the third cow, it walked as if it were animated in the flesh; that it might proclaim to the unbelievers about the grace of God. And that brazen cow walked for four stadia here and there. And all the people who were standing there for the spectacle were seized with astonishment, saying to one another, "Who has ever seen brass that walked like flesh?" And while they were saying these things, they looked and watched whence they should see the blessed one. But as for the cow its brass was melted like water; and it fell to the earth, and the blessed one appeared in the sight of all men. And they were amazed at this wonder. Even the king was greatly astonished that the fire had no power over her. And they all cried to the Lord and said, "There is none like unto Thee, O Lord God, and there are none like unto Thy servants. Be merciful to us as in the abundance of Thy grace. Thou art He who hast done the miracle by the hand of Irene; and Thou hast shewn Thy might and Thy valour amongst the nations." And a hundred thousand souls believed in

f. 132 a God that day. And the few people who were left who were unbaptized, believed nevertheless in God.

And when the king saw that all the people believed in God, he was exceedingly wroth and bitter; and he opened his mouth and blasphemed against God. And he said to Irene, " I swear by all the gods, that I will not spare thee, but I will cut thee up limb by limb ; and I will make thee food for dogs." Then Irene laughed and said, " Thou and thine imaginations shall be confounded, and all thy contrivances against me, thou son of Satan." And when the king had heard [it] he gnashed his tusks like a wild boar against her, and blasphemed God. But suddenly the angel of the Lord struck him with a pain in his heart, and with an internal wound. And he went to his house screaming. And a fire was kindled within him, and he tasted no food, and his liver overflowed and swelled up, and his lung was nourishment for him, and worms came out of his mouth : and his kinsmen were afraid to come near him. And he yelled and burst asunder and died. And his body was decomposed and his bones were scattered. And then the earth did not receive his bones. And when he died, he commanded Bura the Eparch to try the virgin of the Christ. After the death of the tyrant and of those [who were] with him, the word of God had free course by means of the Blessed One ; and God was glorified, and the faith became mighty, and many were baptized. And she was in the city of Callinicus for thirty days doing signs and f. 132 b wonders ; and she cured many in the name of Jesus. She made the deaf hear ; she opened [the eyes of] the blind ; she cleansed the lepers ; and she healed all who were in pain ; and she baptized many in the name of the Father, and the Son, and the Holy Spirit.

And at the end of thirty days the Eparch went to Tela of Mauzalat[1]. And he sent soldiers after her to Callinicus to bring her. And these soldiers[2] found her. And they had heard from many of the citizens the signs and wonders

---

[1] " Mesēmbria " in the Sunaxaristes.
[2] MS. "And the soldiers who went after her to Callinicus."

and miracles which she had done. And they were greatly astonished. And they approached and said to her, "Hail[1] to thee, handmaiden of the Christ! the Eparch[2] sends for thee."

Irene said, "And where is the Eparch?" The soldiers said, "In Tela of Mauzalat, my lady; and he awaits thee there."

And the blessed virgin of Jesus arose, and went with them, and entered the city of Tela. And it was said to the Eparch: "Behold, Irene has come." The Eparch said, "Bring her before me." And she came and stood before him. And when the Eparch saw her, he said, "Peace[3] be to thee, Irene."

Irene said, "Dost thou greet me with peace? but there shall be no peace upon thee. Because God has said, that there is no peace to the wicked." The Eparch said, "Thou impudent and godless woman! Thou dost surely insult me. Approach now and sacrifice to the gods, or dost thou not know that I have received a commandment concerning thee from Numerianus[4] the king to judge thee?" Irene said, "See, and give heed to thyself, lest thou shouldst follow after him who hast commanded thee." The Eparch said, "Approach and sacrifice to the gods, lest I destroy thee from off the world by varied tortures." Irene said, "Hearken, O Eparch, and I will tell thee. We are a spectacle to men and also to the angels. To men for derision, and to the angels for praise. And we are considered as dross by men. Now therefore I say unto thee, O Bura the Eparch! prepare for thyself instruments

Is. xlviii.
22

f. 133 a

---

[1] Or, "Peace."

[2] Properly "Hyparch" *passim*. But as there is no other Syriac equivalent for the Ἔπαρχος of Irene's biography in the Συναξαριστής, we believe that the translator means Eparch.

[3] Or, "Hail."

[4] MS. "the king of Edom."

of torture as thou wilt, and thou shalt see the power
of God in the fortitude with which I shall endure the
agony. But thou wouldst force me to sacrifice to the
lifeless gods, who neither see nor hear, nor smell, nor walk,
whose makers shall become similar to them, and all those
who, like thee, trust in them. And I would persuade and Ps. cxv. 8
advise thee, to turn and to know the living God, who
never dies; He who made thee out of nothing; lest thou
shouldest die a bad death like thy predecessors."

Bura said, "O unmannerly child! O parricide! dost
thou really threaten me?" Irene said, "I have not
insulted thee, but I give thee this advice, that thou
shouldst know Him who kills and who makes alive, who
brings down to Sheol, and who raises up, and who loves
those who return to Him. And I confide in Jesus, that
the grace of the Christ will speedily draw thee, that thou
mayest know God." The Eparch said, "Shall I also then
become a Christian, O cursed child?" Irene said, "I have
said the word, which I know shall become a deed."

The Eparch said, "I swear by all the gods, that I will f. 133 b
not spare thee, nor thy impudence; but I decree for thee
these tortures that have not yet been seen in the world,
nor have they entered into the heart of the judges;
and they will terrify by their severity all who see them."

The Eparch said, "Bring me the smiths." And they
came and stood before him. And he said to them,
"Make me an arm-chair of iron, and let it be one cubit
high in elevation; and make me two thin chains." And
they made [them] and brought [them]. And he commanded them to make Irene sit down. And she came
and stood before him. The Eparch said, "Irene, what
sayest thou? wilt thou sacrifice to the gods or no?"

Irene said, "O Satan incarnate! son of the deceiver!
how far wilt thou persist in thine audacity? Have I not

said to thee that I will not sacrifice to unclean demons,
nor will I worship foul fiends; and I will not forsake my
Lord and my God, Jesus the Christ; and I shall not be
forsaken by Him: for He will deliver me from all thine
inventions, O senseless fool!"

Said the Eparch to his servants, "Make her sit down
in this iron chair, and bind her with these chains, and
heap wood above it. And throw fat and wax and naphtha
and sulphur and pitch and resin upon the wood, and
kindle the fire." And the servants of sin did thus. And
f. 134 a   when the fire had mastered the wood, and had risen above
the chair twelve cubits, the Eparch said, "Let us see if
Jesus will deliver her from my hands." And immediately,
by the commandment of God, an angel descended from
heaven, and seized Irene by her hand, and set her out of
the chair. And the chair and the iron chains were melted
like wax. And he took her out of the flame, and placed
her on one side out of the fire, when the fire had not
reached to her dress. And when the Eparch saw that
she was standing outside of the flame he was greatly
astonished; and he feared and trembled greatly. And
he ran and fell on his face before her feet, weeping, and
sought to persuade her, saying, "I implore thee, O lady,
handmaiden of the Christ, have mercy upon me. Lo! I
also believe in thy God, and henceforth I am a Christian.
And henceforth I renounce all the gods of paganism, and
let me not die a fearful death, lady."

But she said to him, "Did I not tell thee that thou
wouldst speedily turn towards Jesus?" And he said to
her, "I implore of thee, lady, pray for me, that I may be
accepted and not rejected; and that what I have plotted
against thee may not come into judgment against me."
And Irene said, "Peace be to thee, fear not, let no anxiety
come to thee." But when the crowds who surrounded the

Eparch saw that he believed in God, many also believed with him, and confessed God.

And she was there, in that city, for fifty days. And in it she won many to Jesus, and the Lord God sent the holy priest to her in the city of Tela, and he baptized the Eparch and many who were with him who believed in the Lord Jesus Christ. f. 134 b

But Shabur the Persian king had come to Nisibis; and he had heard about the blessed Irene, that she was in Tela. And at the end of fifty days, he sent seven horsemen after her, and they brought her to Nisibis. And when she had entered the city of Nisibis, it was told to Shabur the king: "Irene is come." And he commanded them to bring her. And she came speedily and stood before him. But when Shabur the king saw her, he did not wish to interrogate her, for he said, "This is the destroyer of royalty." And he struck her with the sword which he held in his hand and killed her. The king said, "Is not this the famous one? Why has she not killed me? Where is Jesus her helper? Let him come now and succour her, if he can."

Then the Christian brethren came and carried away her holy body, and buried it. Said the king: "Lest Jesus should come and raise her up?"

After these things the king was silent; and found nothing further to say about her.

And she was for four days in the grave. And at the end of four days, an angel came down from heaven and raised her up. And he said to her, "Irene, thy struggle is finished, and the crown of thy victory is adorned. From henceforth nothing bad shall come near to thy body; and thou shalt see nothing hateful in the world; because the course of thy labour is finished. Rise therefore and enter the city, and fear not; and make disciples f. 135 a of many, according to thy custom. And king Shabur, who killed thee, will do obeisance to thee, and will try to persuade thee to remain in his city. And many will believe in God along with him on account of thee. Blessed and happy art thou among women, and great is thy reward in heaven, and glittering is the crown of thy victory at the marriage supper of the heavenly bridegroom, Jesus the Christ." And the angel went from her up to heaven.

And the blessed Irene took in her hand an olive-branch, and she sang praises and psalms. And she went Ps. lxviii. into the city and spake thus: "Let God arise, and let all I His enemies be scattered; and let those who hate Him flee from before Him," and "There is none like unto Thee, O Lord God! and there are nothing like unto Thy works. For lo! Thou doest wonders to the dead, and men shall Ps. lxxi. arise and praise Thee. O Lord, who is like unto Thee?" 19

And when the citizens saw her, they knew that she had risen from the dead, and they ran and did obeisance before her. And they shouted, saying, "Great is the God of Irene. And there is no other, but He alone." And when there was a shout and a great uproar, the king heard it and was afraid. And he inquired what was the noise of the uproar in the city. The dwellers in his palace say f. 135 b to him, "Because of Irene, who is risen from the tomb, they are thanking and praising God who has raised her." And when the king heard [it], he commanded them to bring her into his presence. And Irene came and stood before him, carrying the sprig of olive, and looking like the dove of Noah, which carried the tidings of peace to the world. Thus Irene also carried the olive-leaf, the tidings of her resurrection. And when the king saw her, he knelt and did obeisance before her. And he said to her, "Irene, great is thy God. And now I know that God dwells with thee. And whosoever opposes thee opposes himself. And

now, lady, I implore and seek to persuade thee, stay in our
city, and do what thou wilt with authority and do not fear.
Because God is with thee, and man is unable to hurt thee."
And she was a long time in that city, teaching the word of
God, and making many disciples. And great was the
praise of God because of her. And the number of all those
who believed in God and were baptized by her hand was a
hundred and thirty thousand souls.

After these things she bade farewell to the king and to
all the citizens; and went to the castle to see her father
and her mother. Ten days before she went thither[1]
Licinius her father died; and she went to the castle and
found him dead[2]. And she was grieved and remained
there for three days. And after three days she bade f. 136 a
farewell to her mother; and arose, and went to the city.
And she left her mother in peace, and was in the city for
three days.

And after three days, by the commandment of God, a
cloud took up the virgin of the Christ, and carried her to
the city of Ephesus, and she was there; and she did many
cures and miracles in the name of Jesus; and she made
disciples of many, for the citizens held her as one of the
Apostles of Jesus. And she was in that city and in its
district for seven years.

And Apellianus her secretary heard it, and he arose
and came to her to Ephesus. And when he saw her, he
did obeisance to her. And they both rejoiced at the sight
of each other. And Apellianus related to the citizens
everything that she had endured from the kings, and they
were very much astonished.

And on the following day she said to all the citizens,
"O brethren and fathers, abide in peace. And be strong

---

[1] Literally, "to the castle."
[2] Literally, "that her father had died."

and firm in the Christ. And persevere and be established in your faith in the Christ. For to-morrow I shall depart. And ye have received me well, and your recompence is preserved in heaven. For ye have heard that our Lord _{Matt. x. 41} said : 'He who receiveth a prophet in the name of a prophet, shall receive a prophet's reward; and he who receiveth a righteous man in the name of a righteous man, shall receive a righteous man's reward and he who receiveth a stranger for the sake of the Christ, the Christ will recompense him in heaven ten thousandfold'." And when she had said these things, she finished her speech. But some of the citizens said, "She has said that she will depart, but where then is she going?" And they said further, "Perhaps she is going to die." Others said, "Nay, but she will ascend to heaven." Others said, "Perhaps Jesus the Christ, her Bridegroom will send and guide her : for we do not know it because we are sinners. God knows what He will do to His handmaiden."

But the blessed Irene said to Apellianus her secretary, "Bring with thee six Christian men, believers, and come with me to a certain well-known place." And Apellianus brought six Christian men of the patricians of the city, and they went with her outside the city. And they found a certain coffin of marble that had been laid there in that place years before; in which man had never before been laid.

And Irene said to Apellianus and to those with him, "Beloved and faithful brethren, abide in peace. Behold! I shall go into this coffin to-day. And do ye take its cover and lay it above it. And for four days let no man come near to the coffin. And she went into that coffin, saying, "Brethren, be at peace; and the grace of our Lord Jesus the Christ be with you all, amen."

And she said, "Let an artificer come and bring iron

clasps, and solder the coffin and also the lid with lead. And mark ye [it] with your signet rings ; and seal it, and go ye into the city."

And she commanded them, saying to them, "When four days are finished, come ye out and open the coffin; and look, if ye find my body in it, well, good; but if f. 137 a ye do not find my body in it, do not doubt, but know ye that my Lord Jesus, my Bridegroom, hath hidden away the body of His handmaiden where He willed. For I know not whither He will carry it ; for I have heard that He said, ' In my Father's house are many mansions'." John xiv. 2

And they did as she had said. And an artificer came and put clasps on the lid of the coffin, and soldered them with lead ; and they all sealed them with their signet rings, and went into the city. And after four days, Apellianus drew near at the time of dawn, he and six Christian men, they with whose signet rings the coffin was sealed. And many of the citizens went out with them to the coffin ; and they bent the knee and prayed there. And they opened the coffin, and they found the clothes of the virgin of the Christ folded up and lying in the coffin. And they did not find her body.

And they saw the angel of God who was standing there beside the coffin. And he said unto them, "Whom seek ye ?" They say unto him, "Irene, my lord, perhaps thou knowest who has taken her away from here." But he said to them, "Lo! she is enjoying herself in the Paradise of Eden, at the marriage feast of the heavenly Bridegroom, Jesus the Christ, the Son of God." And fear took hold of them, and perturbation remained in their minds; and they went into the city praising and blessing God, about the wonder which they had seen. And many who heard it believed, and confessed the name of the Father and the Son and the Holy Spirit. f. 137 b

This is the martyrdom of Irene; this is the conflict of the virgin of the Christ. And she was made the messenger of peace on behalf of all believers.

And the cities in which she triumphed are: firstly, Magedo, the city in which she was born; secondly, Callinicus; thirdly, Tela of Mauzalet; fourthly, Nisibis; fifthly, Ephesus, in which was her good end.

And the kings who judged her: Licinius her father; secondly, Zedekia; thirdly, Severon his son; fourthly, Numerianus; fifthly, Bura the Eparch; sixthly, Shabur the Persian king, he in whose presence she finished the course of her conflict. Praise be to the Christ who gave power to His virgin; and she overcame all the wiles of the devil. May God the Christ give us a portion and an inheritance along with her in the kingdom of heaven! And may her prayer be for the sinner who composed and wrote her martyrology for ever and ever.

Here endeth the story of the blessed Irene.

EUPHEMIA.

AGAIN, the martyrdom of the blessed Euphemia, which took place a mile from the town of Chalcedon, in the days of the Emperor Trajan Caesar.

When Priscus was Proconsul in Europe, there was a great assembly of Christians in the town of Chalcedon. And Priscus the Proconsul had a wicked friend, whose name was Apellianus. And he was a sophist in the f. 138 a erudition of the Greeks. He was a worshipper of Ares. This Apellianus accused the Christians, saying, "O glorious warrior amongst men, and Proconsul wise of heart! let this be known to thy Highness. Because Ares is a great god, so all men should offer sacrifices and libations to him[1] by command of the great Emperor." And this pleased Priscus the Proconsul for the destruction and evil of the souls of those who were enchained in error. And he nailed up placards full of menaces and fierce threats in all the palace of his Highness, which were inscribed after this manner: "Men and friends, citizens of Chalcedon, be it known to you all that it is proper for you to hallow a day, that by command of the Emperor there may be offered a sacrifice to the great god Ares. But if any one should be found who remains in an evil mind, and preaches and teaches the religion of the Christians, I will destroy his body by severe tortures. And let this be the sign to you. When at the time of the sacrifices the horn shall sound

---

[1] Literally, "to the great god Ares."

which assembles you all, ye shall all hasten reverently [and] eagerly to this temple of Ares and offer sacrifices, and know the great god Ares." And every day Apellianus was assidious, that at the time that the horns should sound, and they should move tumultuously before the altar, as was their custom, an investigation should be made about every man as to who had the greatest zeal. And he who blew[1] on the horn blew mightily, and collected all who had lost hope. But the Christians, those in whose souls God dwelt, were all assembled in one house, and they besought God by prayer and entreaty. And the blessed Euphemia was also constantly amongst them, she being the daughter of the senator Philophron. And Drusina her mother was with her. And she was a believer, and did much almsgiving, because she was looking for the hope and the promise of the Christ. Therefore Apellianus, being of the household of Satan, said to the Proconsul: "There are people here who shut themselves up in a single house, who are not willing to obey the commandment of the Emperor, nor the commandment of thy Highness. And if thou shouldst overlook it now, many will turn from the great reverence for the gods, and will go and join themselves to them, and will scatter and disperse our sacrifice with derision." And when the Proconsul had heard this, he commanded them to come into his presence. And when these blessed ones came, Euphemia came in the midst of them with a joyful countenance and in chaste attire, more than all those who were with her, while she illuminated by her splendour the faces of those who contemplated her.

f. 138 b

f. 139 a   And when they came and stood before the judgment seat of the Proconsul, he[2] answered and said to them: "Let all of you be submissive and obedient to the com-

---

[1] Or "called."

[2] MS. "the Proconsul."

mandment of the Emperor, and sacrifice to the great god Ares."

But they all together replied with one voice [and] with the blessed Euphemia, saying, "Be this known unto thee, O Proconsul. We are the servants of the Eternal God, the great King who dwells in the heaven of heavens, and of His true Son, our Lord Jesus the Christ, and of the Holy Spirit. He who hath stretched out the heaven and hath established the earth ; and hath created all works. Him we all worship, being eager to offer ourselves to Him in the sacrifice which is pleasing to Him."

But when Priscus the Proconsul heard [this] he said to them, "I am astonished at each one of you. And I honour the prudence of your mind. Because I have more knowledge ; and I see the loveliness of you all. Therefore be persuaded by me, and obey the Emperor. And take delight in the sacrifice of the gods ; so that ye may have greater friendship from me ; and that the Emperor may take knowledge of you ; and that ye may have greater rank and office."

But when these brave men heard these things, they abated nothing of the splendour which suffused their faces ; but the more were they exalted to the excellencies of the knowledge of God. And whilst the blessed Euphemia f. 139 b was with them, and they were all assembled together in the likeness of a host of angels, they said to the Proconsul, "We, O Proconsul! are the servants of the Most High God ; and we are eager that we may be known by Him in the faith which He has delivered to us ; and that we may receive His promise which says : 'O good and faithful Matt. xxv. servant, thou hast been faithful over a little, behold, I set 21 thee over much.' And also to thee O Proconsul! does it not escape thee, that each one of those who have temporal authority is eager to please him who has given him the authority, that by means of it he may find higher degrees? If therefore it be that those who are mortal and corruptible, are subject unto mortal and corruptible kings, because they receive and seek for transient and unprofitable degrees, how much more should we keep the covenant, which we have made with God, who is incorruptible, and we expect to inherit the promises in His presence, those which endure for ever, which are incorruptible and inalienable. Do therefore what thou wilt, for we are ready because of the expectation of the heavenly promises to give ourselves over readily to death; and we shall receive the treasures that are being kept for us in the presence of God Almighty."

f. 140 a   And when Priscus the Proconsul heard these things he changed his countenance; and commanded that each of them should be tortured with hard and bitter torments. And while these blessed ones were being tortured daily, they endured all the torments for the sake of the Christ, those heroes exulting with joy and encouraging each other to resist bravely in the struggle. And they encouraged the blessed and brave Euphemia that she might attain joyfully to the coronation of her confession of the Christ. And they said to her, "O brave and persevering one! adorn thyself with thy faith, and be courageous in thy sound mind. And like a wise woman who has put on the Christ, receive the victory with all the fathers, whilst thou holdest an unquenchable lamp. Be fortunate in being numbered with the five virgins, those who carried their lamps with joy before the bridegroom, He who will return a full reward in the kingdom of heaven." And when the nineteen days of the labour of the conflict of the blessed martyrs were fulfilled, and they were in the prison nourished by the Holy Spirit; on the twentieth day an idea occurred to Priscus the Proconsul, suggested by the wicked Apellianus, whose mind was also like his name. And he prepared himself for the interrogation of the blessed martyrs. And whilst he was sitting on his judgment seat, he commanded and they called the noble ones, whilst the blessed Euphemia was in the midst of them like a lamp. And the Proconsul asked them, saying, "Tell me, O young men! Have ye felt these tortures and will ye be persuaded to sacrifice to the great god Ares?" And they said to the judge as with one voice with the noble Euphemia: "How f. 140 b long, O Proconsul! art thou possessed by vanity? when wilt thou not turn from the error which has taken hold of thee? that thou mayest know God thy Creator."

Then Priscus commanded those soldiers of Satan to strike the blessed ones on their cheeks and say to them, " Be persuaded and sacrifice to the great God Ares." And the soldiers did[1] as they were commanded. And when they had struck those blessed ones on their cheeks, their faces shone all the more; and those soldiers were powerless, and left off beating the blessed ones, and became as dead people.

And Apellianus, who was of the household of Satan, he who was perfect in the idea of the devil's error, said to the Proconsul, " Pronounce the condemnation of these people, and send them to the Emperor." And this speech pleased the Proconsul and all his companions. And he commanded that they should be cast into the prison-house, and should be kept carefully until it should be the will of the Proconsul that they should be sent to the Emperor. And the number of them all was forty-nine. And the blessed Euphemia was with them also. And when they had come into the prison-house, Sudrinus the disturber and robber came like a thief and like a wolf who fell upon the flock, and snatched away the bravest and strongest of heart,

---

[1] Cod. "did to the blessed ones."

Euphemia alone, imagining that he would find her like a loosened garment. But the beloved of the Christ was covered with joy, and she raised her eyes to heaven f. 141 a saying, "My Lord and my God, Jesus the Christ, Thou art my hope, and let not the work of Thy handmaiden who is before Thee perish."

And when Priscus heard [it] he said to her, "Honour thyself and know the splendour of thy race. And do not thyself destroy thyself: But thou hast been seduced by false words like a woman. Turn now and sacrifice to the great god Ares." But the noble and pure woman said, "The strength of athleticism is not weakened by the weak nature of a woman; but by the preservation of the body the defects of sickness are filled up, for by my nature I stand like a man, that I may be worthy to receive the promises of my fathers."

And Priscus the Proconsul was troubled in his mind that he was overcome by a woman. And he commanded that a machine should be arranged on wheels, and that the blessed one should be thrown amongst them; so that whilst she was stretched out on the machine, and was crushed by it, she should quickly give up the ghost. But when she was thrown amongst the wheels, she marked the sign of the Christ in the shape of a cross on her breast, saying, "O chief of iniquity! how many torments has the enemy of truth poured out in Priscus the murderer? Behold! he sits in accusation and imagines the art of the devil, celebrating the mysteries of his father Satan, as the enemy of the truth. O doer of evil and deceitful man! The torments of thine art do not touch the limbs of my soul; because I have the Christ helping me. And f. 141 b I hope that by means of great and sore tortures I may show to all men the endurance of the struggle whilst I am worshipping."

And when the blessed Euphemia said these things, those soldiers of wickedness turned the wheels upon her. And whilst every one of her limbs was broken with the crushing of the wheels, the health of her soul was longing and was offering thanks to God, saying, "Let Thy goodness and the light of Thy truth be with me. Thou who hidest with Thyself[1] those who call upon Thee[2] in truth, turn to Thy weak and stricken handmaiden and save me from this abyss of that wicked and bad and devilish one, and from the threat of Priscus, this hater of good things."

And when she had said these things, immediately an angel of the Lord descended from Heaven and broke these wheeled machines, and dislocated the limbs of these soldiers, so that they were supposed to be other people from their appearance. And the blessed and victorious one emerged without a single stain. And her cheerfulness was seen in the presence of all men. And the Proconsul said, "By the victorious fortune of the Emperor, and by the good-will of the gods towards us, I swear that if thou dost not sacrifice to the great god Ares, I will destroy all thy body with fire; and thy God shall not help thee, He whom thou dost hope to serve." But the blessed Euphemia answered and said unto him, "This fire with which thou threatenest me, is one which fills up a moment in burning and is immediately quenched. But I f. 142 a am not weak enough to fear thy threats." Then the blessed one answered again and said to Priscus: "Have not these noble champions been thrown into prison for the love of the Christ by thy wicked command? I fear not thy fire, because the Christ is with me. He it is who helps me. But I trample upon thy threats."

And the Proconsul wondered and was astonished at her; and he commanded that the furnace should be kindled

---

[1] MS. "He who hides with Himself."   [2] MS. "Him."

until it should shoot up flames of fire to about forty-five cubits with great strength; and that other soldiers should bring Euphemia. And when they had brought her, she stood up resplendent, with a cheerful countenance and a whole body and said, "Blessed art thou, O God, who dwellest on high, and beholdest in the depth; Thou[1] whom the angels praise, and the archangels worship. I the little, lowly woman supplicate before Thee, because I am persuaded by the excellence of Thy grace, and I seal myself with Thy victorious name; that I may find the redemption of Thy Christ. Thou art He who didst manifest and send Thine angel to the three children in the furnace. And Thou didst scatter from them the strength of the great flames, and didst change the threatening of the Babylonians to peace. Show also to my humility the help that is from Thyself, and deliver me from the mouth of this cruel lion; and from the net of this wicked hunter, and from the threatening of Priscus this Proconsul. For Thy name is glorious and holy for ever."

f. 142 b

And when she had said these things, the Proconsul commanded those soldiers to bind her and to throw her into the fire. And the soldiers bound her carefully. And they laid hold of the blessed one. But one of the soldiers whose name was Sosthenes, whilst he was holding his girdle in his hand, approached the Proconsul and said to him, "Command, O Proconsul, that I be bound with this girdle. For I am not able to stretch out my hand against this blessed one. For behold! I see before my eyes great hosts carrying lamps of light, and looking out for when they may receive her."

And Victor, a soldier who had turned to the knowledge of the truth and had loosened the chains of the blessed one from her, when he said to the Proconsul, "I implore of

---

[1] MS. "He."

thee, O Proconsul, to absolve me from the commandment
of thy violence; for it is hard for me to stretch forth my
hands against this holy one.   For behold! I have seen on
the edge of the furnace men who were standing and f. 143 a
scattering the fire and watching that this blessed one
should be kept without a blemish."

And the Proconsul commanded that those ones should
be guarded, and that other soldiers should stand up.   But
one came whose name was Caesar, and another, Barbessus,
and they caught up the blessed one, and flung her into the
fire.   And immediately the servants of the Only Son of
God received her, the angels holding lamps of the light of
peace.   And they extinguished the flame of the fire.
And that fire turned upon the soldier whose name was
Caesar, and devoured him.   And after the fire had devoured Caesar the soldier of the Proconsul, the blessed one
stood up in the midst of the furnace, as in a beautiful
temple of great glory.   And she saw the Christ our
glorious Lord; and she stretched out her hands towards
Him and said, "Blessed art Thou, O Lord God of my
fathers, who in Thy gracious and passionless Divinity hast
not neglected Thy lowly handmaiden, and hast extended
and exalted Thy true name in every place: and hast
established the splendour of Thy faith.   And hast chased
away the tempest of wickedness; and hast illuminated
and increased Thy righteousness by me.   And in uprightness by Thy Holy Spirit Thou hast charmed away from
us the cursed serpent, and by the skilfulness of Thy many
miracles Thou hast crowned those who put their trust in
Thee.   Grant to me that by Thy will I may triumph
in Thy presence; and that I may be worthy to be numbered
with those who worship Thee in truth."

And when she had said these things, she went out from
the furnace unhurt; being commended to those of the

soldiers who believed in the Christ; the King of truth.

And the Proconsul commanded, "Throw the blessed one into the prison-house that she may be guarded there with the prisoners, till the next day," whilst he was full of his threat of the wicked device as to how he should destroy the handmaid of God. But the blessed one went from his presence to the prison-house, giving glory to God.

And the noble soldiers of the Christ rejoiced in the triumph of the blessed one, and gave glory to God, saying, "Blessed be Thou, O God! for ever and ever, Amen. Grant to Thy servant, O Lord! that she may be worthy to testify with all the fathers, those who were worthy to be martyred and were put to death for the sake of Thy holy name."

THE SECOND INTERROGATION OF EUPHEMIA.

Again on the following day the Proconsul went forth and sat on his judgment seat; and he commanded them to bring Sosthenes and Victor before him, the soldiers who believed in the Christ. And he said to them, "Sacrifice to the gods." But they answered and said to him, "O Proconsul, we have surely erred from of old by the instigation of the enemy of mankind, whom thou worshippest; and for a certain time we have worshipped him, and we have destroyed our hope towards the true God. But we believe now in Him who has enlightened the dark eyes of our heart, by means of His handmaiden the blessed Euphemia. Who is able to wipe out the record of our debts. He who was with us in the trouble of the enemy of the truth, we believe that He is able to inscribe us [as]

citizens of the Holy City, in the Book of Life. Do then what thou wilt with eagerness, the works of thy father Satan, and torture us, because we do not assent to thine error, and we do not receive the commandment of the

Emperor, who commands that he be worshipped ; because he is a servant of the living God, and we do not worship impure and false gods."

And when the Proconsul had heard these things from them, he commanded that a [bear ?] should come, and that the blessed ones should be thrown to it, so that their bodies might be devoured by it. And the two were immediately thrown together to it. And they began to speak thus, and to give glory to the Lord Almighty, the Pure and Holy One. " He who hath established all works with wisdom ; · and by His powerful word assembleth the host of the seas; and by His commandment He hath established the earth ; and He hath separated the darkness from the light ; He who slew the murdering dragon, and loosed the bands of death by the murder of the Crucified One. Loose us also now from the pangs of corruption ; and deliver us from the laceration of the manslayer, and grant to us that we may honour Thy holy name in peace without blemish and without spot of soul or of body." And immediately there was a voice from heaven, saying, " I have heard your prayer, and have received your intercession." And these ones, when they heard the voice, committed their souls the more to God. And when they were thrown to the wild, destroying beast, they immediately f. 144 b committed their spirits to God, and received Him whom they loved with joy, because of whom the blessed ones had died[1].

And when the Proconsul saw what had happened to the blessed ones, he arose immediately and went to his Praetorium. And the Christians, who happened to be there, took the bodies and wrapped them up and buried them[2] in the earth in a fair covering.

---

[1] Literally, "had been crowned."
[2] MS. "their bodies."

And when it was dawn, the Proconsul arose, and went out that he might go and hear the blessed Euphemia. And when she emerged from the prison-house, she went like an innocent lamb of the Christ and said with a clear voice: "I give Thee glory, O Lord! with a new song upon this earth. I extol Thee, O Lord! with all my strength, I sing a psalm to Thee, giving glory to Thy name amongst all peoples." And when she had prayed and had finished, she came and stood before the judgment seat of the Proconsul.

And the Proconsul began to interrogate her, saying to her, "How long wilt thou be a fool? and how long wilt thou destroy thyself in this manner? for the great god, the Emperor, desires to be reconciled to thee, if thou wilt also do his will, and wilt sacrifice to Ares, to whom he also sacrifices. Be persuaded therefore by me and sacrifice, that thou mayest live. And in the world thou shalt be a mother of many." But she laughed, and f. 145 a answered, saying to him, "Truly I would have no mind and no sense, if I were to do what thou desirest; and were to hearken to the Emperor, and to worship those who are no gods by nature, and were to sacrifice to those dumb and voiceless idols, O wicked and senseless man! and were to renounce all the beauty that is in the Christ, and were to rush into the snare of Satan. Thou art eager to make me in thy fashion like unto thyself, who art the heir of hell and everlasting quenchless fire. And thou pervertest the servants of God from the truth. For the strength of the Christ is with me, and I believe that He helps me at all times."

And the Proconsul commanded that they should bring four great stones, and should fix great instruments at the corners of the stones, and that the blessed one should be thrown into the midst of them. And when these stones were shaken by the instruments by being moved to and fro, they should tear the body of the blessed one.

And the instruments were arranged, and he commanded that she should go in amongst them chained. And when the lamb[1] of the Christ went in amongst these stones, she knelt on her knees, and implored with many tears and besought God, saying, " I beseech Thee, O Lord my God ! and I pour out my soul before Thee, prostrate before Thee and I offer my lowliness, and I shed my tears, my back is ready for smiting, and I withdraw not my face from spitting. I call upon Thy name, and I take refuge in Thy true fear. Have mercy upon Thy handmaiden, and leave me[2] not to this destruction which the craft and wickedness of the evil one has prepared against me. I may be stripped of all wicked things, my thoughts shall be purified from uncleanness, men shall be amazed at Thy help ; let not his wiles have power on the spiritual cymbals of my soul. Let my purity[3] shine, O Lord ! in the world, that Thy name may be glorified for ever." The noble woman said all these things while she was kneeling in her prayer. And the lictors worked till they were wearied, hanging on the contrivance of the wheels, and not one of them moved from its place ; but they and the wheels became like fine chaff. And she was found as a lamb without blemish ; and the judge and those who were with him contemplated the brightness of her face. And after all these contrivances which they had sought out in wickedness, the judge commanded them to dig a deep place, and to surround it with water as with a wall, and to cast evil beasts therein ; and to shut up the noble woman there, and when the beasts should leap from the water, they should destroy Euphemia with vehemence.

Isa. 1. 6

f. 145 b

---

[1] MS. " Calf." [2] Literally "her."
[3] Or "victory."

And when the blessed one knew it, she was prepared
for the place, and the waters were pressed together; and
the beasts were flung in before the wicked man commanded it.

And the holy Euphemia ran, and stood on the edge of
the lake of water. And she sealed herself with the sign of
the cross, and said to the judge with a loud voice, "O liar
far from the truth! wily man, disciple of Satan, thou art
well called by this name, saws (driven by) water are
prepared for thee, which when they receive thee with
anger, shall dislocate all thy limbs; because thou hast
embittered the God who made thee, the Giver of life and
f. 146 a   light, and hast contemned the worshippers of the Christ.
And when the blessed one had said these things, she
signed herself with the cross on the right hand and on the
left, and cried to God her deliverer. And she looked up[1]
to heaven, "O Christ the light of my soul! be with Thy
handmaiden to-day, and deliver me as Thou didst deliver
Daniel in the den, and like Jonah in the belly of the fish."

And when she had finished speaking, she threw herself
into the midst of the water. And when all these beasts
perceived her, they ran to meet her with joy; and they
carried her and lifted her up above the water. And they
rocked her like a nurse her darling, for they were greatly
restrained by the fear of God.

Then when the Proconsul saw the great and powerful
miracles that had happened, he said to Apellianus, the
pagan and sophist, "What is that power? and who is it
that helps this woman? for as I have seen, the demons
obey her, and she conquers every one by her sorceries."
The Proconsul said, "And how do the gods endure to see
these things, and they do not take vengeance."

---

[1] Literally "stretched her look."

Apellianus said, "Because in their mercy they do not take vengeance."

The judge said, "Let swords and sharp stones be fixed in the earth, and let no[thing] be seen above them. And when Euphemia comes confidently, and is walking as on plain ground, she will trample on the swords, and will fall there on the stones and die like a wild boar." He commanded therefore, and his soldiers completed the contrivance of the wicked one. And when they had completed the arrangement according to the commandment of the Proconsul, the blessed Euphemia came with joy and cheer- f. 146 b fulness, as one who had borne all these things, and yet did not fail of the truth of Jesus the Christ her Lord. And when she had borne all these afflictions, while these soldiers of wickedness were provoking her, that she might run to that place, the angels snatched her up and transported her over that place quite unhurt, and those soldiers fell into what they had fabricated for the blessed one ; and they died by the work of their own hands.

And again the blessed one opened her mouth and gave glory and said, "Thou God, knowest what is in the hearts of all, Thou art He in whose presence are all secrets. O Giver of treasures that cannot be spoiled, and of heavenly promises, Who hast stretched out the earth and established it upon nothing, and by Thy word hast appointed all works. And Thou hast created the light, and caused it to shine upon all. Thou[1] who by Thy good-will didst send Thine only Son, our Lord Jesus the Christ from heaven to loose the bands of death ; and to bind and to subjugate the chiefs and the worshippers of error. Thou[1] who art near to Thy worshippers, to those who stand in the conflict for the sake of Thy name. And Thou art a helper to them in all their

---

[1] MS. "He."

afflictions. Help Thy handmaiden also now, and by the
prayers of those blessed and holy ones who have been
thrown into the prison because of Thy divine name[1], and
are hoping to finish their divine course, deliver me also,
Thy handmaiden, and keep me in the one harmony with
Thy Holy Spirit, because Thou art God. For Thou
keepest not anger and Thou dost save in the times of
affliction."

And when the Proconsul saw these things, he commanded them to bring the holy woman before his judgment-seat. And he answered and said unto her, "Dost
thou know, O Euphemia! that whilst thou art of a very
great and distinguished family, thou hast been led into error
and hast remained in it until now? And I who am a
governor keeping what is right for the Emperor, thou
standest against me, truly, like a wise and skilful woman.
But nevertheless now at least be persuaded by me. And
forgive me these insults and torments which I have made
thee endure, and sacrifice to the gods, and be not a
reproach of all men; and remain in thy distinguished
family."

But the blessed one, because her mind was established
in the Christ, answered and said to the tyrant, "Why do
I see that thy face is full of bitterness and guile? O
workman who composes with ornamented words! O
wolf clothed in sheep's clothing while he does the works
of destruction! and wicked robber, proffering words that
are sweet to hear, but in their sequel they are more
bitter than wormwood. I am not foolish to such a
degree, that I should leave Him, the treasure of life, and
should be allied to the bitterness of the devil. Therefore
be not deceived, O Proconsul! because thou canst not

f. 147 a

---

[1] Literally "the name of Thy divinity."

persuade me to sacrifice to foul fiends; and thou canst
not force my will, that I should call those gods who
are no gods. For how can they be called gods who have
never been so? and how dost thou not perceive that thou   f. 147 b
comparest with the life that is eternal a dead thing which
never existed, and commandest us to offer a sacrifice
to it. I am not persuaded by thy words, which are full of
bitterness. Be eager therefore and do what thou wilt;
for I am eager that I may be made worthy by means of
thy wicked wiles of the everlasting victory. Where the
Father is, where the Creator of the angels is, where the
Giver of the crowns of victory is; there is the anointing
of the truth; there is also the Christ who crowns His
champions; there is also the Holy Spirit, He who
strengthens those who endure afflictions for His sake."

And the Proconsul was angry when he heard these
things, and he commanded that they should scourge the
blessed one with rods, saying to her, " Be persuaded, and
sacrifice to the gods." But whilst she was being scourged,
she spake thus:

" Thy tortures do not come upon me, O wicked man!
Thou art parted from life and thou hast no permanent
abode. For thou art weak, because thy tyrannical power
is conquered."

But Apellianus and the Proconsul with him recollected
in their mind; and the judge commanded that they should
bring sharp saws and pans of fire, and that the saws
should, by the construction of their instruments cut up the
blessed one and fling her limbs into the pans of fire, that
thus she might be pounded to pieces like fine ashes. And
when those instruments were arranged in that manner   f. 148 a
of contrivance, they brought the blessed Euphemia, and
threw her amongst the saws, and the saws were turned
about, and were scattered; also the pans of fire that were

fixed amongst them were quenched, and no hurt came
to her from any of these things, because the angels of
God kept close to her for her assistance. And when
the Proconsul and Apellianus his friend saw that this worshipper of the Christ was victorious over all their afflictions
and torments, they took counsel amongst themselves how
they might destroy the holy one, and they invited the
city to the theatre which is called the arena where beasts
are let loose for the Stadium. And when she stood
in the midst of the Stadium, she began to say, " Thou
art near, O Lord! to those who call upon Thee in
truth. Receive my spirit to Thyself, as Thou didst receive
the sacrifice of our father Abraham; so also do Thou
receive the sacrifice of my spirit to Thyself." And whilst
she said this, she sealed herself on all sides, calling on the
name of the Father and of the Son and of the Holy Spirit.
And four lions were loosed against her, with two other evil
beasts. And these lions leapt upon her with a run. And
they kissed the foot-prints of the blessed one. And the
other beasts did so likewise. And thus was finished the
martyrdom and the conflict of the blessed one. One of
these beasts ran, and bit her on her shoulder only : and
f. 148 b immediately a voice was heard a voice from heaven
saying, " Ascend on high O Euphemia! climb and stand
in the place of the saints, and receive thy victory, and
the reward of thy finished course."

And when this voice was heard, there was a great
earthquake, so that all the place was shaken, and every
one was seized with trembling. And the blessed one said,
" Requite, O Lord! also this unclean Proconsul according
to his wickedness, and enter into the conflict along with
Thy holy servants, O Thou, my God and my Lord! and
justify them." And when she had said these things, she
committed her soul into the hands of her Lord. And her

father Philophrōn entered with her mother; and they took her holy body, and carried it far away, and they buried it in a lonely place, which they had arranged for it, which was about one mile distant from the city of Chalcedon.

And the Proconsul sent those blessed ones who had been thrown into prison with the Blessed One to the Emperor with an epistle; that the Emperor might command whatsoever he willed about them. And he commanded those cavalry soldiers that they should convoy them peacefully on the way; and keep them until they should go before the Emperor. For the Proconsul fell into a sore sickness, and was bitterly tormented according to the word of the Blessed One which she spake to him.

Here endeth the martyrdom of the Holy Euphemia.

SOPHIA.

THE Memoirs of the noble women who were crowned in their martyrdom for our Lord, of Pistis, and of Elpis, and of Agape, and of their mother Sophia in the city of Rome.

By the grace of God was the gospel sown abroad under the heaven throughout all the earth, by Jesus Christ the Saviour of all men; that every man might believe in God the Almighty: and in Jesus the Christ the Only Son, and in the Living and Holy Spirit, and that every man might be drawn away from the worship of idols, and from vain error; and that they might receive help for their souls by the baptism of holiness for the remission of sins.

And when this word was preached by the Apostles, and by all the Evangelists, all regions ran joyfully and kissed the feet of the Apostles in faith. For many and noble were the doctrines of the truth and by means of them we have all come to the right way.

And there was a certain woman of a great family of the house of Sallustius; and her name was Sophia. This woman went up to the city of Rome, with her three beautiful virgin-daughters; and they hoped to receive the sign of the Christ our Redeemer. And her daughters had been reared in wisdom and in the grace of God. And their mother rejoiced greatly and gave glory to God, when she found His love[1] in the heart of her daughters. And she prayed to her Lord that He would send help to His handmaidens. And whilst these virgins were strengthened f. 149 b in the fear of God, and were constant in prayer and in vigil, it was known by the mind of all men that they were shewing the life of the martyrs and of the Apostles in the years of girlhood. For they went according to their custom on the first day of the week to pray in the house of God. And of a sudden Satan disturbed the heart of Add. 17,204 Antiochus (one) of the rulers of the city; and he said f. 23 b in the presence of the Emperor Hadrian, "A certain woman and her three daughters—whence they are we know not—are teaching the women every day to worship one God, and His Son Jesus the Christ, and that we should become strangers to our wives: for they touch neither food nor drink, and they do not go away from these virgins: and thus they are separated, that they may even wipe out the praise of our gods from the earth."

And when the Emperor Hadrian heard these things he sent the guards after them; and they laid hold on them, and brought them to the palace of the Emperor. And these faithful women, the virgins of the Christ, went joyfully with their mother, holding each other's hands, and when they had arrived at the door of the palace, all of them made the sign of the cross on their breasts. And these virgins were so beautiful that none of the onlookers was able to come near them and look on their faces; but they only contemplated (them) as in a mirror. And the f. 150 a grace of God was also poured out upon the virgins. Add. 17.204 f. 24 a

And when they had entered the palace and stood before the Emperor, he raised his eyes to look at them and at the loveliness of their faces, because he wondered at the

---

[1] Literally "the love of God."

glory of their beauty, and at that moment he was unable to interrogate them. But after a little while he came to himself, and he replied and said to their mother, "Who art thou, O woman? and whence comest thou? that thou hast thus disturbed all Rome? for thou hast denied the gods, the governors of the whole world. And what is thy name, tell us?"

She returned an answer and said, " I am a Christian."

The Emperor said, " I did not ask thee this, but 'What is thy name?'"

And the handmaiden of God returned an answer in truth, " The people who gave me birth called my name Sophia; but the full name is 'I am a Christian,' of the stock of the chiefs and nobles of the city of Italy, but the mercy of the Christ has redeemed me and my daughters and brought us to the city of Rome, that I may present before Him the fruits which His grace has given me, and may present them with joy an offering to the Lord."

And when the Emperor heard these things he commanded that she and her daughters should be with one of the chiefs until there should be an interrogation. And the faithful woman Sophia gave counsel to her noble daughters, saying, " Hearken to your mother, my beloved daughters, I reared you (in what concerns) your stature, and I taught you all letters. Now the hope for which ye look, and the grace which ye love, calls you to Him. Look not at the childishness of your years, nor at the superb beauty of your faces. Clothe your mind with heavenly armour, and be strong with the breastplate of the Spirit, and place a crown upon your mother by your endurance. Withstand the persecutors. And for your sakes, my beloved ones, my soul may be purified from iniquity. For if ye go before me, and stand in the presence of the Heavenly King, it will be known to all

Add. 17,204
f. 24 b

f. 150 b

men in the kingdom of heaven, and those who please
God will present me for your sakes, and I shall be with
you in the life that never passes away.   My beloved
daughters, the hidden darlings of the foster-mother, and
the fair nestlings of my womb, have pity on your mother
who has endured pains because of you : and be strong and
firm before the tortures of the persecutor.   Confess one God,
and the Lord Jesus Christ, and the Living and Holy Spirit,
for He will repay you with the crowns of endurance.

" Hearken to me and wonder.   Woe is me ! "

And when the mother had sowed these sayings in her
daughters, they were strengthened by the Holy Spirit, and
were the more filled with wisdom.   And the one encouraged the other and filled the other with wisdom.   And
every hour they made (the sign of) the cross of the Christ
on the breasts and between the eyes ; and they were
constant in prayer and intercession, and were longing to   Add. 17,204
receive the crown of victory.   And they said to their   f. 25 b
mother in concert, "O mistress of daughters, the blessed
mother of us all, let not thy mind doubt concerning the   f. 151 a
faith of thine offspring[1].   But offer joyfully the children
of thy womb to God.   And thou shalt behold our endurance and our confession.   For the Christ our Redeemer,
the teaching of whose scriptures is in our minds, He who
beholds from Heaven, adorns us with wisdom and with
faith ; and gives us a response in the presence of the king
in judgment."   And when their mother had heard the
readiness of their heart she said, "I gave birth to you
three, my beloved daughters, listen to the voice of my
words : The life of this world is for a short time.   May
the most loving of mothers strengthen your minds a little,
may the kingdom of heaven be yours ! and I will follow
you joyfully in the pride of my mind, and with the praises

---

[1] Literally "fruit."

of my soul, and I will offer to God the perfect sacrifice of
your victory."

And after three days the Emperor commanded that
they should bring them. And when these virgins went
their mother also followed them joyfully. And when they
entered the palace, and stood before the judgment-seat of
the Emperor, he answered and said to the three noble
sisters, "O lovely girls! lo! I see your beauty, and I
contemplate in the likeness of your faces that it is not
approaching to the nature of man, but it is another glory,
which is in its light like the brilliance of the sun. I
also see your stature, that ye are of very tender years.
Therefore I counsel you to have mercy on the old age
of your mother and on the desirable vision of your appearance. Be persuaded by me, as by a father, and sacrifice
to our lords, the gods, and if ye hearken to my word,
and offer sacrifices to the gods, ye shall be called the
daughters of the king. Ye shall find bliss and luxury:
and ye shall have fame like the daughters of the king.
For the Eparchs shall enter my presence, the governors
and the chiefs, all the senate shall be summoned, and all
the armies of my dominion, and a deed of adoption shall
be signed according to the law.

"But if ye will not submit to me, nor hearken to my
word, ye shall be delivered up to bitter torments. I will
fling the beauty of your faces, and the pride of your limbs
to the dogs. Therefore submit to my words before all
these things come to pass. For because ye are of a distinguished race, for this reason ye shall be called the
daughters of the king."

The glorious virgins replied and said to the Emperor
with one voice, "Thy promises are very vain, and they are
not necessary to the handmaidens of God. We know Him
who has brought us up, God the King of the worlds, the

f. 151 b

Maker of heaven and of earth, of the seas, and of the
depths below, that He will receive us as beloved children.
For the armour of our conscience is formed from our
youth and our mind is made strong in hope. There is
a power within us to withstand against thy devices, and to f. 152 a
conquer all thy interrogations, and we shall enter joyfully
on the road to the skies[1], and the door of heaven will
be opened before us; and we shall enter joyfully and shall
worship the King, the Christ. Produce therefore all thy
tortures, that by the trial of our endurance the long-
suffering of God, and of Jesus the Christ, our Redeemer,
may be made known; for He will help His handmaidens
in the conflict." Then the Emperor was filled with rage,
and called Sophia, the mother of the maidens, and said
to her, "What are your daughters called? tell me their
names, and tell me their ages."

And their mother answered, saying, "The name of my
eldest daughter is Pistis, twelve years old. And the name
of the second is Elpis, ten years old. And the name of
my youngest daughter is Agape, seven years old. And
these names being interpreted in Aramaic, are Faith,
and Hope, and Love. And the name of their mother is
Sophia; which being interpreted, is Wisdom." And the
Emperor answered, saying to Pistis, who was the eldest of
the[2] sisters, "Sacrifice to the goddess Artemis, whose
interpretation is Beltis; and contemplate her appearance, for she is the patroness of Beauty." And Pistis
(Faith) answered, saying, "O the blindness of man's mind!
Shall we forsake the God who made everything by His
word? and Jesus the Christ our Redeemer? And shall f. 152 b
we worship senseless idols, and speechless stones?"

And when the Emperor heard these things, he com-

[1] Literally "the height."
[2] MS. "her."

manded that they should strip her of her clothes, and should scourge her with rods until she should sacrifice. And when twelve men scourged her by turns, not a scar was found on her body. And when the Emperor saw that no stripes were visible on her body he commanded them to cut off the fountains of her milk with the sword. But the great crowd who were standing for the spectacle saw the tender age and the beauty of the maiden who received these tortures; and they all wailed, weeping and saying, "These maidens have been judged iniquitously. The punishments of the Emperor are bitter, and his commandments are unjust." And when the breasts of the maiden had been cut off, they threw them on the ground before her eyes. But the places from which they had been cut off flowed with milk instead of with blood. And when all the crowd of the Romans saw these wonders, they gave glory to God. And the virgin of the Christ said to him, "O judge, thy tortures are very slight, and my limbs do not feel thy scourges. And even the members which have been cut off from me, instead of running with blood, are fountains that flow with milk. And I pray much that by means of the devices of thy imaginings I may be confirmed in the knowledge of the

f. 153 a Christ. Hearken therefore, O unjust man, O wicked disciple of Satan, for if thou hast commanded that they should disfigure even the image of my face, not even thus will I be frightened, for thou wilt be punished for all these things in the day of judgment. But I stand for the truth of my faith, and I do not deny my Lord."

Then the Emperor commanded, and they brought a gridiron of iron, and they kindled a fire below it, until it was all aflame. And they brought the faithful one, and threw her on the top of the gridiron. And the noble virgin was like a ship on a calm sea, which the storms do not touch. And she prayed with a loud voice, saying, "O Lord the Christ! look upon the low estate of Thy handmaiden, and give me the victory over the fiery flame. And preserve me spotless before Thee; may I resist the devices of the persecutor."

And when three days had passed away, whilst the girl was lying on the top of the fire (and she never ceased praying), the Emperor commanded that the gridiron should be taken away, and that a frying-pan should be set up instead of it, and that they should throw oil and wax, and f. 153 b pitch into the frying-pan. And when they were thrown together into the frying-pan, it[1] boiled and flamed with the burning of the fire. But the noble woman looked [up] to heaven, and cried to Jesus the Son of God, and before the king had commanded she threw herself into the midst of the frying-pan; and immediately the flame was quieted, and the fire was quenched; and the frying-pan froze like ice; and the handmaiden of God was glad there, and despised the devices of them all. For God helped His handmaiden. And when the Emperor saw that she had not died with all these tortures, and was not persuaded to sacrifice, he was much grieved, and meditated by what means he should destroy her. And he thought that he would slay her with the sword. And when she had heard that the king had commanded thus, she besought her mother joyfully to pray without ceasing, that the commandment of the Emperor might be speedily fulfilled. And the noble woman said to her sisters, "O beloved ones! daughters of the same womb, beloved of a faithful mother! ye see Him whom our souls have confessed, and before f. 154 a whom we must stand. Be strong therefore in witnessing for our Redeemer. For we have been brought up in the doctrine, and one mother has given birth to us all. And

[1] Literally "the frying-pan."

lo! she rejoices in the endurance of her offspring to-day, and she prays that she may behold our victory. Therefore do not let us make God angry, nor vex the love of our mother, who has borne pain and distress, and pangs and groanings for us one by one, and we have sucked the same milk from [her] sacred breasts. And we have learned wisdom and the discipline of God. And behold! by grace we are drawing near to inherit eternal life. And I am going in a beautiful path; and I pray that ye may come beside me by the same path, in joy and in perfect love. But henceforth, O my sisters, do ye walk in the steps of your sister, that together we may receive the promises of the Only Begotten, in the kingdom of heaven."

And when she had finished speaking, the daughter embraced her mother, and kissed her reverently, and she besought her to offer prayer on her behalf: and she did likewise to her sisters. And she made herself ready for the slaughter; and stretched out her neck to the sword. And her mother and her sisters encouraged her, saying, f. 154 b "O sister of her mother, and mistress of her sisters! approach joyfully to the consummation and be not afraid of the sword. Go fearlessly on the path of life, and we will walk in thy steps. We will fearlessly withstand the persecutor; and we shall overcome all his devices. We will come and precede thee on the road to the skies. Be praying for us, O our sister. The road on which thou hast gone is greatly to be desired. Thy Lord in heaven waits for thee. Remember us also in the kingdom of heaven, us thy sisters Elpis and Agape. Pray that we may see thee speedily."

And again her mother said to her, "I gave thee birth, my daughter, and thou wast reared upon the milk of my breasts; and I endured many distresses for thy sake. Go joyfully on the everlasting road. Go, and see the heavenly light, and prepare a bright place for thy mother, and remember her who bare thee, O my daughter!"

And when the sword was about to fall upon the neck of the maiden, she stretched out her holy hands to heaven, and prayed with a loud voice, saying, "Glory be to Thee, O Lord Jesus the Christ, that Thou hast deemed Thy little handmaiden worthy to withstand in the conflict of the noble ones. I beseech of Thee, O Lord, remember Thy servants and Thy handmaidens, and the little ones, and the great ones, the rich and the poor. Remember, also Thy handmaiden, my blessed mother, and my beloved f. 155 a sisters who worship Thee. Remember me also, O Lord, Thine afflicted and sinful handmaiden, and receive my soul into Thy presence because I have confessed Thy cross. But do not forgive the wicked man, the persecutor, the unjust Emperor. But may he be requited, with indignation and with ruin, and with Thy rage and with fire in this world; and receive the spirit of Thy handmaiden in peace." And when she had finished speaking, she stretched out her neck, and received the sword with joy. And she wore the crown of the victors. And her mother came joyfully, and embraced the body of the noble woman, and kissed her, and she praised God with a joyful heart.

But the Emperor Hadrian sent for her second sister, whose name was Elpis. And he counselled her, saying, "My daughter, be persuaded by me as by thy father, and worship the goddess Artemis; and remain alive and do not die."

And the noble woman, Elpis, answered, saying, "Thou knowest, O Emperor, that thy counsels are very useless, and they do not touch the handmaid of God. For behold! thou hast learnt by the interrogation that I am the sister of the blessed Pistis. And we have sucked the

same milk. And we had the same training in doctrine.
And we are ready to go on the one road, and henceforth
do not deceive thyself with many words, but do what thou
hast willed to do. For I have hoped in God, and He is
the stay of my soul, and from Him is the crown of my
victory; and my mind will never swerve from beside Him,
and to Him my thoughts reach."

And when the Emperor had heard these things, and
had seen that he was gaining nothing, he commanded
them to strip the girl of her clothes, and to scourge her
with ox-hides. And those who scourged her were changed
to the number of ten men; and those men striking her
became tired.

And her mother stood, saying, " Lord Jesus the Christ !
give patience to thy handmaiden as to her elder sister."
And when her mother had said these things, Elpis said
with a loud voice, " O Lord God ! before Thee I pour
out my tears. Give me patience, that I may receive the
crown of my victory." And to the Emperor she said,
"O most wicked of men ! what dost thou meditate concerning me ? Produce thy tortures quickly, and by the
very proof thou shalt see who is helping me."

But the Emperor meditated cunningly in a great rage
as to how he should destroy her; and he commanded that
she should be cast upon burning coals. But when she was
thrown upon the fire, she walked on the top of it. But the
Emperor did not see those who were helping the girl.
And she raised her voice and said, " O Lord ! turn not Thy
face away from Thy handmaiden, but grant me that I may
be made perfect before Thee in the endurance of my mind;
and may the unjust Emperor be requited with ruin, and
with the worm that never fails."

But when the Emperor had heard these things, he
commanded that they should hang her on a tree, and

f. 155 b

f. 156 a

destroy her with combs. And whilst the noble Elpis
was being combed, the flesh from her sacred limbs fell
away, and was fragrant and pleasant, as (with) choice
scent, and she stood with a cheerful countenance. And
the blessed one laughed and said, "O wicked, bad man!
as it appears to me as if on thee the combs are descending, for I do not feel them; nor will I be persuaded
to sacrifice." And he commanded again that a cauldron
should be put on the fire, and should be filled with
wax and pitch and fat and resin, and that they should
kindle fire beneath it; and should throw the girl into
it. And when the cauldron flamed from the kindling
of the fire, drops from it were leaping, and they carried f. 156 b
the maiden that they might throw her into it. And at
that moment the copper was melted, and it fell as wax
is melted before the fire. And it burnt up all the unbelievers who were standing round. And the Emperor
was not softened with all these things, but when all his
devices were overcome, he commanded that she also should
die by the sword, like her sister. And when the girl heard
that the decree was issued, she ran to her mother and
saluted her, saying, "O blessed mother, peace be to thee!
and be mindful of thy daughter Elpis." She ran again to
the body of her holy sister and embraced and kissed her.
And she approached again to her youngest sister, and
kissed her and embraced her, saying, "My darling sister,
and daughter of my beloved mother, come beside us
speedily. For I also am going on the road to eternity.
My darling sister and daughter of the same womb, and
beloved of a believing mother, do not fear the tortures of
the unjust man. For He who has given us freedom, He
will send us help. He is the Father of the truth. He is
the true Lord." And when she had said these things, she
said again in prayer, "O Lord God, hearken unto Thy

f. 157 a handmaiden in joy and in peace." And her mother had said in the joy of her heart and in pride about the victory of the girl, "My darling sweet daughter Elpis, go with joy on the road to eternity, and be mindful of thy mother, for I gave thee birth." And when her mother had finished saying these things to her, the blessed one bent her neck, and went away by the death of the sword.

But her mother rejoiced while she contemplated the crowns of her daughters, and she kissed their[1] corpses and said, "I have sent acceptable heralds before me to the House of Life."

And she turned towards her youngest daughter, saying, "Agape, my daughter, the most beloved of her sisters[2], be strong and vigorous. Behold I see two crowns prepared for thy sisters, and on the head of them both the crown of thy childhood appears, and I am hoping to go on the road of thy victory. And henceforth be thou strong in the name of our Lord Jesus the Christ."

Then the tyrant called the girl Agape, and interrogated her with words. And the noble woman returned an answer, saying, "O wicked man and tyrant! dost thou not know that I am the sister of these two who withstood thee in the struggle, and received the faith and the crown of

f. 157 b victory? For one father and one mother gave birth to the three; and we sucked one milk equally. We were educated in letters and in wisdom, and we increased in glorious knowledge. And because of this it is fitting that we should conquer together in the struggle." And when the mother had heard these things she said, "Thou hast well spoken, my daughter. Be strong, and resist with vigour. And gird thy loins with the confession of the Most High." And when the Emperor[3] had heard these

---

[1] Literally, "the corpses of her daughters."
[2] sic in Cod.   [3] MS. "he."

things, he was filled with a great rage. And he roared like a lion for the prey. And he was altogether merciless. And he commanded that she should be stretched out with rods, and that the combs should be brought close to her body, that while they were dripping and tearing from all sides the limbs of the girl should be torn; but the damsel did not feel the combs, but her eyes were strained towards heaven.

And he commanded again that after the combs they should scourge her with rods. And whilst the girl was being beaten[1], she said, "O tyrant Emperor, why dost thou tire (thyself) uselessly? for I do not feel thy tortures." And when the Emperor heard (this) he commanded them to loose her, and prepare a fiery furnace, that she f. 158 a might be flung into it. And when the furnace had been kindled for three days, it glowed more than the light of brass by its flame. And when the Emperor came to the furnace, and saw that it was kindled, he commanded them to bring the girl. And she came and stood before him, and he answered and said to her, "I request thee to say one sentence, 'Great is the goddess Artemis.' And when thou shalt have thus spoken, thou shalt speedily escape from this distress."

The noble one answered and said, "O senseless fool and ignorant dunce! what dost thou chatter about? for because thou hast cut off thy hope from life dost thou make these promises?" And the Emperor, in a great rage, commanded that she should be flung into the fiery furnace. And before they had seized her, she entered the furnace joyfully. And in that very hour the fire flew out from the furnace to the length and the breadth of sixty cubits; and the worshippers of idols, six thousand, died of the flames. But the faithful one walked inside the

---

[1] Literally "swallowing them."

furnace, and praised God, saying, "I extol Thee, O Lord! the preserver and saviour of Thy[1] handmaidens, take pity upon me, according to Thy mercy, and deliver me from the hand of the slayer." And when the Emperor heard these things, he was again filled with a great rage. But the flame escaped from the furnace, and burnt up his body, and flung him upon the earth; and the life hardly

f. 158 b remained in him; and it was dashed about greatly by the burning. And he sent the guards after the noble woman, that they might bring her again before him. And when they arrived at the door of the furnace, they saw three men within it, whose raiment was like snow, the light of their faces was like the radiance of the sun, the hair of their heads was like gold; and they walked with Agape in the midst of the furnace. And these guards fell down on their faces from fright: and in their distress they said to the noble one, "Come out from the furnace, for behold! the Emperor wants thee." Agape came out, and went and stood before the judgment-seat. And he commanded that they should heat an auger in the fire, and pierce the body of the faithful one with it. And when the wicked man saw that she despised the many tortures, and contemned the afflictions, and overcame the fire by prayer, he commanded that she should die by the sword. The noble one opened her mouth and said, "O Lord Jesus the Christ! I thank Thee and I praise Thee, that thou hast deemed me worthy of the victory of noble men, with my two sisters; and hast called me to the delight of Paradise. And now I beseech Thee, O Lord! remember

f. 159 a Thy people who worship Thee. Remember also the faithful Sophia, my mother, who has stood before Thee with joy, and has served Thee splendidly, and on account of that make her worthy to remain three days in the world,

---

[1] Literally, "His."

and when she has made a memorial to her daughters on the third day, may she also be crowned with her daughters, and be buried beside us victoriously. And when Thou shalt do this, O Lord! we three sisters will praise Thee, and the faithful mother, and we shall be a memorial to Thy name for ever."

And Sophia prayed to God, and said to Agape, "My most beloved daughter, go with joy in the path of Thy Lord. For I pray for this, that I may offer three virgin crowns an offering to the Lord; and may be remembered by my daughters in the kingdom of heaven. For lo! I see thy crown which is perfect in the host of the noble ones."

And when her mother had finished saying these things to her, the noble woman stretched out her neck, and received the sword with joy.

And her mother Sophia embraced and kissed the bodies of her three daughters, and clothed [them] splendidly, and she yoked a carriage and placed her daughters upon it, and she went out of the city to a certain place that is eighteen miles from the city. And she placed the bodies of her virgin daughters there in a high place carefully; in the holy temple of their victory. And on the third day she went out to the cemetery that she might carry spices according to the custom. And all the free women of Rome went out with her, and also a great crowd of men and of women. And she poured out spice on the bodies of her daughters, and made a great commemoration according to the custom. And when all the crowd were standing, she offered a prayer, with sobs to God. f. 159 b

And when she had finished praying, she stood before the bier of her daughters. She opened her mouth and said, "My beloved daughters, I also am going with you, and I shall be worthy of the crowns of your promises."

And when she had said these things, in that same hour

she committed her soul to God, and slept the sleep of rest. And the rich women who were near, placed the blessed Sophia in the coffin of her noble daughters. And they went together to the Lord, and inherited life eternal.

Hadrian the unjust Emperor perished with many pangs. For the pupils of his eyes fell out, and the flesh perished from his bones. His legs were cut up by worms, and his hands from his joints, matter came out of his mouth, and he was altogether ruined. He cried with a loud voice, saying, " O Lord God, who didst help the three maidens and their mother, take my soul from me. For I know certainly that I bear this because of these three lives." And when he had said these things, he wailed with a loud voice, and burst in twain. His flesh was scattered from him, and his bones were not found. And this happened to him by prophecy, for his wickedness.

Here endeth the martyrdom of Sophia, and of her three daughters.

f. 160 a

CYPRIAN AND JUSTA.

AGAIN, the martyrdom of Cyprian the wizard, and of S. P.
f. 170 a Justa the virgin.

At the appearance of our Redeemer, Jesus the Christ from heaven upon the earth, and on the fulfilment of the words of the prophets, everything beneath the heaven was illumined, that they might be baptized into one God the Father Almighty, and into the Lord Jesus the Christ, and into the Holy Spirit in the belief of the truth.

Now there was a certain virgin whose name was Justa, and the name of her father was Aedesius; and of her mother Cledonia, in the town of Antioch which is near Daphne. And this blessed one listened to a certain deacon whose name was Praylius, from a window which was near her house. And when she heard the great deeds of God, and how our Redeemer the Lord Jesus Christ put on a body, and the heralding of the prophets, and His birth from Mary, and the worship of the Magi; and about the appearance of the star and the praise of the angels, and the signs of the miracles that were done in His name and by His power; and of the redemption of the cross; and of Add. 12,142
f 74 a His resurrection from the dead; and of His glory in the presence of the disciples; and of the living words of His gospel to His apostles; and of His ascension to Heaven; and of His being seated on the right hand; and of His imperishable kingdom; and of the bliss that passeth not away, and of the deathless life.

[And when the blessed one had heard these things, she

marvelled greatly in the belief of the truth, and the eye of
the maiden sparkled with the love of the Holy Spirit.
She longed greatly and sought that she might again see
the deacon Praylius; but she could not (do it)[1].] She
answered and said to her mother, "Hearken to thy
daughter, my mother, and turn from error, and thou shalt
escape from everlasting torment; as thou hast heard that
the scriptures of our Lord Jesus Christ say, He who hath
made the heaven and the earth and all that is therein.   For
sculptures are nothing.   They are of stone, and of wood,
and of gold, the work of men's hands, images, deaf, and
blind, and lifeless."   Then her mother said to her, "Nay,
my daughter, let not thy father hear this in thy thoughts."
But the blessed one answered and said to her mother,
"Know ye, O my father and my mother, that henceforth I
am a Christian, and I worship the Christ my Redeemer,
because by means of this deacon I have learnt the way of
life.   And henceforth there is no God except the Father,
and the Son, and the Holy Ghost.   And He gives life to the
men who believe in Him, and He has redeemed them from
the destruction of the wicked, and has made them to inherit
deathless life."   When she had said these things, she signed
herself in the Threefold name, and began to pray in the
name of our Lord Jesus Christ.   But her mother told her
father everything that the blessed one had said.   Then
immediately numberless hosts of angels appeared to them,
holding lamps of fire in the chamber[1].   And in the midst
of them they saw the Christ, saying, "Come to Me, I will
make you enter the kingdom of heaven.   With all the holy
ones who have done well in My presence."

And when Aedesius, the father of the girl, saw that
sight, he was seized with great wonder.   And he arose in
the morning, and led his wife, and his daughter, the blessed

Add. 12,142
f. 74 b

---

[1] From the Sinai palimpsest.

one, and they went to the church with that deacon, be-
seeching him to present them to the bishop. And when
he presented them, the Bishop received them. And they
fell at his feet and besought him that he would give them
the seal of the Christ. But he was unwilling to give
it to them, until the deacon related to him about the
vision of the Christ which he had seen, and about the faith
and the love to the Christ of the maiden.

But Aedesius shaved his hair because he was a priest
of the gods ; and he fell at the feet of the Bishop, and
he gave to the three the seal of the Christ. And the holy
Aedesius was deemed worthy of the priesthood, and he
lived a short time, and went to rest in the true faith. And
the holy virgin went at all seasons to the church of the
Christ. But a certain man, a lawyer of a great family,
who was evil in his deeds, and who was enchained in the
worship of error, of dead images, saw the blessed one
going at all seasons to the house of God. And when he
saw her, he was captivated by the love of the maiden, and
he sent many people after her, that he might take her to
wife. But she said to them all with a loud voice, " I am
betrothed to the Christ." And the wicked man, by the
mad impulse of Satan, assembled a great crowd, and
watched her as she went to the house of God. And he
wished to lead her away by force. And when they came
to lead her forcibly away, those who were with the maiden
cried with a loud voice. And when those who were in
their house heard these things, they came out grasping
swords. And those who had come to seize the handmaiden of God by force, fled.

But the holy one sealed herself with the sign of the
Christ, and she seized the insolent man and flung him on
the ground. And she struck him on the face. And she
tore his clothes and left him stupified, as her sister Thecla

had done to the insolent Alexander. And she went forthwith to the house of God.

But he went in a great rage to Cyprian the wizard, and
promised him two talents of gold, if mayhap he might
entrap the holy maiden with his sorcery, whilst the
madman did not know that the power of the Christ is
unconquerable.

But when Cyprian the wizard had heard these things,
he was grieved for the young man, and called up a certain
cruel demon by his sorcery. And it answered and said to
him, "Why hast thou called me?" And Cyprian said to
it, "That I may please a certain maiden of the Galileans,
if thou canst bring her to me."

But the demon, ashamed, promised that it would bring
her to him, whilst he was unable to conquer the truth.
Cyprian answered and said to it, "Tell me, what are thy
works, in which thou confidest, and I will send thee away."
The accursed demon answered and said to him, "I am
a rebel against God, and I obey Satan. And I made
Eve to sin, and I have driven Adam out of Paradise.

Add. 12,142
f. 76 a

And I have robbed him of bliss and of delight. And
I have taught Cain to kill his brother. And I have
polluted the earth with blood. And I have increased
adultery and sorcery. And I have made all lasciviousness
and drunkenness. And I have incited silly laughter. And
I have taught men to worship images. And I have
counselled that the Christ should be crucified. And I
have shaken the whole city. And I have overturned
walls. And I have divided houses."

And when the demon had said these things that had
been done by it, it said to the wizard, "I have done all
these things, and am I unable to conquer this?" Then
Cyprian said to him, "Take this root and sprinkle it round
about the house of the maiden. And I will take her mind

away from her, and immediately she will obey thee." And
when he had said these things to the demon, he went
straight to the house of that maiden. But the blessed one
stood up to pray the None in the night to God the lover of
the penitent. And when she became aware of the arrival
of the demon, she prayed all the more to the Living God,
because her mind was satiated with the love and the power
of the Cross, and she signed herself with the sign of the
Christ. And she called with a loud voice, saying, "O
Lord, Almighty God! Father of our Lord Jesus the
Christ, [1]Thou who didst kill the man-slaying serpent, and
didst deliver those who were bound by Satan, O Lord
God! who didst create man in Thine (own) image, and
didst leave him in the paradise of delights to enjoy himself
in Thy commandments,—and he was thrown down by the
deception of the serpent. And when he sinned thus Thou
didst not forsake him, but by the power of Thy cross
Thou didst cure his wounds, and didst make him whole,
by means of the Christ, the Redeemer of the worlds, He
by whom the created things were made, and the heavens
were set in order, and the earth was stretched out ; and
the waters of the great deep were separated, that all
natural things should confess to Thee, O God! O Lord
Jesus the Christ, redeem Thy handmaiden ; and let not
the temptation of the enemy come near me. To Thee,
O Lord! I have made a vow that I would be a virgin to
Thine only Son, the Lord Jesus Christ. Redeem Thy
handmaiden, because I have loved Thee and will love
Thee, with[2] all my heart, and with[2] all my soul, and with[2]
all my strength. Thou, O Lord! hast made the light of
Thy love to shine on my soul. I beseech Thee, O Lord!
leave me not to the hands of the Wicked one, that I may
not transgress the promise that I have made to Thee.

Add. 12,142
f. 76 b

---

[1] MS. "he." [2] Literally, "from."

Chase away the thought of the rebel from my mind; and keep me in Thy truth." And when she had said these things, she signed herself with the sign of the Christ, and she puffed at the demon; and he went away ashamed; and he stood before Cyprian; and Cyprian said to him, "Where is the woman for whose sake thou hast been sent?" The demon answered and said to him, "Do not ask me, for I cannot tell thee. For I saw a certain sign and I have run away." But Cyprian laughed at him; and he again called by his sorcery a stronger demon than the first one. And the cursed one boasted, and said to Cyprian, "I knew thy commandment and also the cowardice of him who was before me. Send me O my father! and I will do thy will."

And Cyprian said to him, "Take this root, and throw it outside the house of the maiden, and I will come and persuade her." And when the demon had come to the place which Cyprian had told him of, the handmaiden of God stood up to pray the Sext of the night, saying thus, "At midnight I have arisen, and I will praise Thee for Thy righteous judgments. God of all! Lord of the heights and of the depths, who hast confounded Satan by Thy power, and hast put him down under the feet of Thy disciples. May the confirmation of Thy mercy remain with me, O God! who didst receive the sacrifice of Abraham; and didst hear the prayer of Daniel; and didst overthrow Bel, and didst slay the dragon; and didst shew the knowledge of Thy divinity to the Babylonians, God, who by means of Thine Only Son, the Lord Jesus Christ, didst dispose everything, and didst bring out everything that was concealed in darkness to the light; and didst bring to life even those who were dead. And now, O Lord! in the abundance of Thy grace neglect me not, O Merciful One! but keep my soul and my body near to

Thy holiness. Keep also the lamp of my virginity, that it may not go out; that I may enter with the Bridegroom, the Christ, to the marriage feast; and may commit to Him my virginity in purity and holiness."

And the demon went away from her ashamed, and appeared to Cyprian. And Cyprian answered and said to it, "Where is the woman on whose account thou hast been sent?" It answered and said to him, "I cannot tell thee. For I saw a certain sign and I was afraid, and ran away." S. P.
f. 173 b

Then Cyprian called one whom he thought to be stronger than they, who was the father of the demons, and said to him, "Who is this slight thing by whom thy power has been conquered?" The demon answered and said to him, "I will bring her to thee, be ready at once." Cyprian answered and said to it, "What is the sign of thy victory?" The demon answered and said to him, "I will enfeeble her with much fever for six days, and at midnight I will make her ready for thee."

And the demon went and appeared to the maiden in the form of a maiden, her companion. And it went in and sat down on the bed as if it had been a woman, and the evil one began to talk to the handmaiden of God in the manner of penitence. "I beseech thee, O handmaiden of God, receive me, that I may be with thee. The Christ, thy Lord, hath sent me to thee. For I also am a virgin like thee, and shew me what is the struggle for virginity, or what recompense there is to those who keep it in purity. For I have seen thee that thou art greatly afflicted in the conflict." Add. 12,142
f. 78 a

But the holy maiden, the servant of God, answered and said to her, "The tongue[1] of man cannot describe the reward of the virginity which is for the sake of the Christ;

---

[1] Literally, "mouth."

for it[1] is very great. God has promised to those who love Him and preserve their virginity, what eye hath not seen, nor ear heard, nor hath it arisen in the heart of man. Who is able to comprehend the blessings which God has promised to those who love Him and preserve their virginity in purity? The struggle for virginity in this world is for a little while; but the blessings which are preserved for it in that world are neither transitory nor corruptible."

Add. 12,142
f. 78 b

But the wicked demon began to speak with guile to the handmaid of God, saying to her, "Behold, I have heard that Eve was a virgin in Paradise, and was not blest. And when Adam had known her, and she had given birth to children, she received the knowledge of good and of evil. And by her means the world was peopled; and there was the succession of races and of tribes."

But when the holy virgin heard these things, she rose up to pray because of the words of the crafty one. And the cursed fiend kept close to her, lest perchance there might be an opportunity for him to capture her. But the blessed handmaid knew the craftiness of Satan, and was much troubled because she had perceived that he was a deceiver; and she hastened to prayer in the presence of God. And she sealed herself with the sign of the cross. And she puffed at that demon in the power of Jesus the Christ. And he fled ashamed from beside the hand-maiden of God, and went sadly to him who had sent him. But the holy one was strengthened by the power of the Christ, and rested from the dispute with the crafty one, and gave thanks to God who had helped her in the struggle. And straightway the fever left her. And she

Add. 12,142
f. 79 a

began to say, "Praise be to Thee, O Christ! who strengthenest those who seek refuge with Thee and who

---

[1] Literally, "its reward."

dost illuminate (with) Thy glorious beams those who are blind in the darkness of evil, Thou, O Lord! in the abundance of Thy mercy, deliver me not up to be vanquished by a stranger to righteousness. But help Thy handmaiden who hopes in Thee. For my flesh shudders for fear of Thee, and I have been afraid of Thy judgments. Give glory to Thy holy name, that those who hate me may see and be ashamed. For Thou, O Lord! hast helped me, and hast comforted me with Thy threefold power."

And the demon had gone and had appeared to Cyprian the wizard. And it replied, saying to him, "I too, have again been vanquished by one weak woman."

Cyprian answered and said, "Where is the power of thy victory? tell me." The demon answered and said to him, "Ask me not, for I am unable to tell thee. For I saw a sign and I was shaken and fled. But if thou art willing that I should tell thee the truth, swear to me, and I will tell thee."

Cyprian answered and said to him, "What have I that I can swear by to thee?"

The demon said, "Swear to me by the great power that abides with me."

Cyprian said to him, "No, by thy great power, I will not go away from thee."

And the demon had become trustful and said to him, Add. 12,142 f. 79 b "I saw the sign of Him who was crucified. And I shook, and I was afraid, and I ran away."

Cyprian said to him, "Is therefore He who was crucified greater than thou art?" The demon said, "Be patient and listen to me and I will tell thee truly. All that robs and deceives is allied to us, and becomes our comrade in that fearful place. For that torment is bitter. For they boil copper and place it on the limbs of both men and women.

And thus by hard boiling they are[1] tortured before the tribunal of Him who was crucified. And the angels also afflict them with severity."

Cyprian said, "Therefore I also wish that I could be a friend to Him who was crucified; that I also may not fall into His hard condemnation."

The demon said, "And hast thou not sworn to me by my great power that thou wilt not deal falsely?"

Cyprian said, "By what have I sworn to thee and have dealt falsely?"

Saith the demon, "By my great power."

Cyprian said, "I reject thee and I scorn thy great power. For this night I have surely learned that I can take refuge in the prayer and the intercession of a virgin. And I supplicate by the power of the cross. And by it all thy lying power is humbled. For I also sign myself with the cross, and deny thee and all thy power."

And when he had spoken thus, he sealed himself with the sign of our Redeemer, and said, "Glory be to Thee, O Christ! O invincible Power!"

Add. 12,142
f. 80 a

And immediately Satan fled.

And Cyprian said, "Henceforth I believe in the Christ, and He redeems from all the power of the Evil one."

But the demon went away ashamed. And Cyprian took the tablets of his sorcery and made the four men of his household carry them; and thus he went to the house of God; and he fell at the feet of the presbyter Euthymius[2], and said to him:

"O blessed servant of God! I implore thee that I may become a soldier of God and of our Lord Jesus the Christ; and that I may be inscribed in the book of the believers—those who serve Him." But the presbyter Euthymius imagined that perhaps he was seeking to deceive

---

[1] MS. "he is."   [2] Syriac Palimpsest "Anthimus" *passim.*

those who were in the church. So the holy one said to Cyprian, "Let it suffice thee that thou hast deceived so many people who are without. Take heed to thyself, and do not come into the church of God with guile. For the power of the Christ is invincible."

Cyprian answered and said, "Of a truth, my lord, I, too, know that it is invincible. For this night I sent demons against the holy virgin Justa. And she conquered them by her prayer and by her love to the Christ. But take the books of my sorcery, with which I have done all the evil, and burn them in the fire. And take pity on me, and let me belong to the flock of the Christ." Add. 12,142 f. 80 b

And when the holy Euthymius had heard these things from that wizard, he took his tablets and burnt them in the fire. And he blessed him and began to say to him, "Be constant in the house of God at the time of prayer."

And Cyprian went to his house rejoicing; and he broke all the images that belonged to him. And all night he beat his hands on his face and on his breast, saying, "I have dared to withstand Thy power, Lord Jesus the Christ! in all the wicked things that I did. And how may I bless Thee with the mouth wherewith I cursed the men who called upon Thy name." And he threw dust upon his head, and flung himself on his face upon the earth, and wept for seven days. And after the seven days, he got up early as great Saturday began, and he went to the house of God. And as he was going on the road, he said in his prayer:

"O Christ! O Helper of those who call upon Thee in truth! If I am worthy to become Thy servant, shew me some place where I may enter Thy holy house, and may hear from the reading of Thy holy scriptures, O Lord! Add. 12,142 that Thou hast received me." f. 81 a

And when he had entered the house of God he heard

Ps. xxxv. 22   the chorister[1] say, "Thou hast seen (it) O God! be not silent." And then, "O Lord! be not far from me." And
Is. lii. 13   again he heard Isaiah who said, "Behold my servant shall deal prudently, and shall be exalted, so that many
Ps. cxix. 148   shall be astonished at him," and again David saith, "Mine eyes have prevented the watches that I might meditate on Thy word."

Is. xliv. 2   And again Isaiah has said, "Fear not, O my servant Jacob, and Israel, whom I have chosen." And again the
Gal. iii. 13   Apostle, who says, "The Christ hath redeemed us from
Ps. cvi. 2   the curse of the law." And again David hath said, "Who shall relate the wonderful works of the Lord?" And again
John iii. 16   the Gospel, which hath said, "That whosoever believeth in me should not perish, but should have eternal life." And again they proclaimed, "That whosoever did not receive the sign should go out." And Cyprian sat at the threshold of the door, and one of the deacons said to him, "Rise and get thee out." But Cyprian answered and said unto him, "I am a bond-servant of the Christ; and thou sayest to me, 'Get thee out!'"

Add. 12,142   And that deacon said to him, "Thou art not yet initi-
f. 81 b   ated, Cyprian." And Cyprian said to him, "As the Christ liveth, He who confounded the demons, and hath had mercy on me and on the maiden, I will not go out until I am initiated." And Asterius the deacon went and informed the Bishop. And the Bishop called Cyprian. And he repeated to him the words of the holy scriptures. And he prayed, and thus he baptized him in the name of our Lord Jesus the Christ.

And after eight days he became a preacher of the hidden mysteries.

And when it was Pentecost, he was full of the grace of God, and healed demons and pains in the name of

---

[1] Or "the Psalmist."

Jesus the Christ. And until one year was completed, he became the assessor of the Bishop. And for sixteen years he held the sacred throne. And after these things the holy Euthymius summoned the Bishops who were round about, and said to them things that were worthy of the Church of God, and he, while still living, gave him the throne of the bishopric. And after a few days, the holy Euthymius went to rest in the Lord[1], and confided to him the flock of the Christ. For the holy Cyprian had put many things in order, and had made the holy Justa a deaconess, and he enlightened many, and delivered them from all the heresies of destruction; and increased the Church of the Christ; fulfilling the words of the prophets, fulfilling also the commandments of the Christ, whilst he laboured concerning the belief of the truth. He looked on the people who were scattered, and on the wolf whilst he was robbing.

Add. 12,142
f. 82 a

And the holy Cyprian taught many (people) of the city by letters. But the Lord of evil, crafty Satan, incited the sons of error to calumniate the holy one before Eutolmius, Count of the East, and they said to him, "Cyprian is the teacher of the Christians; and he makes void the glory of the gods by his many sorceries, with a certain virgin, and disturbs all the world by his letters, and makes women virgins."

And the Count was filled with rage, and he commanded the judges to bind Cyprian and the maiden carefully, and to bring them to the city of Damascus and produce them before him. And when they had come before the Count he said to them, "Art thou the teacher of the Christians? who of old hast turned away many from the praise of the gods, and hast deceived many by Him who was crucified? exalting Him more than the gods?"

---

[1] Literally, "Christ."

But the holy Cyprian said, "Why hast thou given thyself to the likeness of wickedness? and to the madness of the evil one? For I, as thou hast said, was captive to the enemy of justice, whilst I was the teacher of the pagans; and I slew many by every kind of sin. And when the Christ redeemed me, He helped me also by means of this maiden. A certain lawyer from the house of Claudius fell in love with her. And when he could not find (a way) to do evil to the handmaiden of God, desiring to capture her for his wife, he came to me and begged me to do the business of love for him. And I, confiding in the books of my sorcery, sent the demons against her. And she made them flee by the sign of the Christ. And thus (it was) until the third one. I even sent their chief, and that holy maiden overthrew them by the same sign of the Christ. And when I saw what had happened, I adjured that demon that he should tell me for what reason he could do nothing with the power of the maiden. And when the demon was burnt by the angel he told me all the truth. And he said to me again, I am the discoverer of all bad things. And I recollected myself and gave the tablets of my sorcery to the Bishop, my predecessor, whilst all the chief men of the city were present. And he burnt them in the fire. I would also persuade thee now to withdraw thyself from the madness of images, and come to the house of God, and thou shalt know the power of the Christ, which is invincible."

Add. 12,142
f. 83 a

Then the Count was enraged against the blessed one. And he commanded that he should be hung up and combed. Also concerning the holy virgin, he commanded that she should be beaten[1] with rough thongs on her face; the two being hung opposite to each other. And the maiden began to say, "Glory be to Thee, O true Christ!

---

[1] Literally, "swallow."

that Thou hast brought me who am unworthy near, to fulfil Thy will. And I am beaten[1] because of Thy name, which exalts its worshippers." And when the lictors were weary of beating the blessed one, she praised God all the more.

Add. 12,142 f. 83 b

But the Count commanded them to cease from her. And when Cyprian was being combed he did not feel the combs.

The Count answered and said to him, "Sacrifice and escape from the tortures, and thou shalt not die miserably."

The holy Cyprian replied and said to him, "Why dost thou exalt thyself against God and withdrawest from Him? and dost not wish to draw near to the gospel of the Christ? For thou wilt not keep me back from the path of life. For I am running that I may attain to the heavenly-minded who inherit the kingdom, and may be made worthy, by means of those tortures which thou art bringing to me, of bliss that can never pass away."

The Count said, "And wilt thou inherit the kingdom of heaven because of these tortures? I will bring greater ones than these to thee."

And he commanded that they should conduct him to the prison-house, and the holy Justa with him. And he commanded that they should be guarded with diligence. And when they entered the prison-house, it shone by the grace of our Lord Jesus the Christ who was with them.

And after a few days the Count commanded that they should bring them before his judgment seat. And the Count answered and said to the blessed ones, "Do not be deceived by the faith and the sorcery of a mortal man, and lose your lives."

Add. 12,142 f. 84 a

But Cyprian answered and said to him, "This death has won eternal life for those who love Him."

---

[1] Literally, "I swallow."

The senseless Count answered and said, "Heat the frying-pan and throw into it pitch, and wax, and bitumen, and fling the blessed ones into it[1] when it boils." And when they had thrown him in, he was not at all hurt.

Then the Count commanded, and they brought the blessed Justa to the frying-pan. And when she drew near, the Evil one cast fear into her mind, and she began to be afraid. But the blessed Cyprian cried and said to her, "Come, O handmaiden of God! for thou hast shown me the path of life; and thou hast opened to me the door of heaven; and thou hast shown me the glory of the Christ. Thou hast been strengthened against the demons. Even their chief thou hast reckoned as nothing by the power of the cross. And how shouldst thou fear the fire."

And the blessed one signed all her body, and ascended into the fiery frying-pan. And both of them rejoiced and exulted in the frying-pan as amongst refreshing dew.

Add. 12,142
f. 84 b

And Cyprian answered and said, "Glory be to God in the highest, and peace on the earth; and goodwill to upright and faithful men." And he said again, "Because Satan is fallen from heaven, and is trampled beneath the feet of all those who believe in the King, the Christ, our Redeemer. For He hath bound the Evil one in darkness and all who obey him. I praise Thee, O God! for all in which Thou hast deemed us worthy to suffer contempt for Thy sake. I implore of Thee, O merciful Lord, to receive our sacrifice for a sweet savour of Thy greatness."

And the Count heard, and laughed, and said, "I curse you and all the skill of your sorcery."

And Athenus his colleague and profane friend said to the Count, "Let thy Highness command me, my lord, and I will approach the boiling pan in the name of the gods; and I will overcome the great power of the Christ."

_____
[1] Literally, "the frying-pan."

And the Count said to him, "Approach." And when he approached the frying-pan, he lifted up his voice and said, "Great is the god Zeus! and the father of the gods Asclepius, who giveth health unto men." And when he came near to the boiling of the flame he fell, and all his limbs were split like wax before the fire. But the grace of God preserved the holy Cyprian and the maiden without a spot; because they praised God.

Add. 12,142
f. 85 a

And the Count was troubled and said, "What shall I do? He who was my priest and friend has died miserably. What I shall do to these wicked people I do not know." Terentinus answered and said to him, "Have nothing to do with these people whom thou dost call wicked. And do not withstand the truth. For the power of the Christians is invincible. But send them to the Emperor, shewing him the matter of their crime."

And the Count wrote the report about it thus:

"To the great Emperor Cæsar, who ruleth by land and by sea, Diocletian, greeting. Against the commandment of thy Majesty have these men arisen. And I have apprehended them: Cyprian, who is the teacher of the Christians, and the virgin, who is named Justa. And from the reports, my lord, thou wilt learn into how many tortures and afflictions I have thrown them; and they would not be persuaded by me to obey thy laws, my lord, and I have sent them to thine august Majesty." And when the Emperor had read these reports about the blessed ones, he was greatly astonished at their endurance, and his friends implored him and said to him, "Do not withstand the great power of God."

Add. 12,142
f. 85 b

And when the Emperor had heard [it] he said: "To Cyprian who is the teacher of the Christians with the virgin Justa, who have chosen the vain heresy of those who are called Christians; and have forsaken life, and

have chosen death.   Therefore I command concerning
them, that their heads be taken off with the sword.

And while the blessed ones were being led off to death,
to a certain place in which they were to reach their consummation, they asked the lictors that a little time might
be given them, in which they might pray.

And the holy Mar Cyprian began to pray, saying,
"Remember, O Lord! Thy Church, in every place, and all
Thy faithful and true servants, and be Thou near to those
who love Thy name."

Add. 12,142
f. 86 a
And he made the sign of the Christ over his whole
body, and he placed the virgin Justa on his right hand:
and he persuaded these lictors that she should be beheaded
before him.   And so the lictors did.

And the holy Cyprian said, "Glory be to Thee, O
Christ, the Strengthener of Thy worshippers!"

And a certain great man was there whose name was
Theoctistus, a faithful man; and he approached and
greeted the holy martyr as he was being slain with the
sword.   And Balbus, the colleague of the Emperor, commanded concerning him, that his head should be taken
off with the sword.

And when they had been crowned, and the blessed
Theoctistus with them, the bodies of the blessed ones
were thrown to the wild beasts.   And they did not
approach them for many days.

But a sailor, a certain faithful man, when he heard
about the end of the holy ones, because he was a kinsman
of Theoctistus, took faithful men of his own with him.
And he made them sit for six days and six nights, until
they had snatched away the corpses of the blessed martyrs
Add. 12,142
f. 86 b
from the custodians, because the bones of the blessed
ones were much more precious to them than gold, or silver,
or costly pearls.   And they carried them to the city of

Rome with their memoirs. And they gave them to a certain woman whose name was Rufina, of the distinguished family of the Claudians. And this faithful woman Rufina carried the bones of the holy martyrs and laid them in an honourable place wrapped in pure linen, and with fragrant spices. And every one who approached the blessed ones received health and help from them.

And these things were done in the consulate of Diocletian, in the city of Nicomedia, on the fifteenth of the month which is called Haziran, our Lord Jesus the Christ reigning in heaven and on earth.

Here endeth the Martyrdom of Cyprian the wizard, and of Justa the virgin, and of the faithful Theoctistus.

HYMN.

Again, verses of Mar Ephraim, from the Hymns of Paradise.

The assembly of the saints, in the type of Paradise.

. . . . . . My brethren, the life-giving cluster maimed the serpent, held captive by the curse. Eve's mouth was sealed in the silence of help, while again that mouth (reproached ?) her Maker.

Blessed is he who is worthy to be in Paradise, when the glorious fruits of the trees abound.

And again they ought to look at the fruits of the noble ones; flowers . . . . . are conquered; they who see the pure and holy blossoms of their crowns; joy of the creation and its Creator. (They) please Him who knoweth all the fruits of righteousness, more than the fruits and berries of the trees. The beauty of nature praises Him; it praises the intellect. Paradise (is) knowledge; the flowers the deeds; the garden the freedom; the earth the mind.

Blessed is He who exalted Adam.

Blessed is he who is worthy to behold their robes.

Blessed is he who is worthy to listen to their wisdom.

Blessed is the ear that is drunk with their voices.

Blessed is he who learns to be amongst the foremost ones.

Woe be to him who does not even press that he may not be the last.

One of them cleft the air in his chariot. The angels desire to meet him, for they saw of late a body in their dwelling. And as the earthly form in the chariot ascended, thus our Lord descended clothed in a body by His grace; and being clothed in a cloud, He rode and ascended to reign above and beneath. Angels of fire and of wind wondered at the Elijah whom they saw, for in Him was hidden the gentle wisdom. On earth they wondered at . . . its Creator, and they saw the Virgin and they rejoiced.

Thou hast made the low things great and hast astonished the high things.

They offered her in the midst of the earth her crown in Paradise.

Whosoever never utters the curse of vituperation, he has a desire more than . . . and he who is chaste . . . some beauty shall be seen by him . . . his thought . . . .

. . . . f. 181 a

Praise be to the Father and to the Son, and to the Holy Ghost, now and always, and for ever and ever. Amen.

Here endeth this book of the Select Narratives: first, of the blessed Thecla; second, of Eugenia; third, of Pelagia; fourth, of Marinus; fifth, of Euphrosyne; sixth, of Onesima; seventh, of Drusis; eighth, of Barbara; ninth, of Mary; tenth, of Irene; eleventh, of Euphemia; twelfth, of Sophia; thirteenth, of Theodosia; fourteenth, of Theodota; concerning the Faith; fifteenth, of Susan; sixteenth, of Cyprian and Justa; seventeenth, verses about Paradise.

°⸪° I, the mean one, and the sinner, John the Stylite, of the monastery of Beth-Mari-Qanūn (Conon?) in the town of Ma'arrath (Mesren[1]) Kaukab of Antioch, by the [mercy] of God, I have written this book for the profit of myself, of my brethren, and of those who are neighbours to it; but because of [the love] of the Christ, I would persuade all those who [read] in it to pray for me the more [earnestly] . . . . But whenever thou meetest with this book . . . concerning the sinner thy prayer.

This book was finished in the year a thousand and nine[ty[2]] of Alexander of Macedon, the son of Philip, in the month of Tammuz[3]: on the third day of the week, at the . . hour of the day, of the Baptism of our Lord Jesus the Christ. May . . . for the sinner who wrote this book . . . the multitude on the Right Hand. Amen, and Amen, and Amen.

[1] From Professor Bensly's transcript of f. 165 b.

[2] Doubtful. A hole occurs here; and it may possibly have contained an ornamented flourish.

[3] *i.e.* July.

THIS IS THE BOOK OF THE SELECT NARRATIVES
ABOUT THE HOLY WOMEN.

INDEX OF PROPER NAMES.

L. E.

The name "Jesus," which occurs frequently in these tales, is not included in the above list.

"Ḳaddisha" and "Qanūn" have the same initial letter in Syriac, and I regret that I am constrained to represent it by two different letters in English. I have retained "Ḳaddisha" because I wrote it thus in my Introduction to the text of the Four Gospels from the same manuscript; and I prefer Qanūn with a Q in order to distinguish it from "Kanūn," the name of a month. There is always a difficulty in transliterating the letter ܩ into English.

CAMBRIDGE: PRINTED BY J. AND C. F. CLAY, AT THE UNIVERSITY PRESS.